ЧтениЯReadings

Chtenia: Readings from Russia

**a themed journal
of fiction, non-fiction, poetry,
photography and miscellany**

Cover photo: *A Thought Tied Up in a Knot* (Yevgeny Maximyuk)

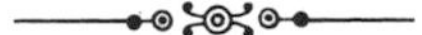

ISSN 1939-7240 • Volume 4, Number 4 • Issue 16
Chtenia is a quarterly journal of readings from Russia, including fiction, non-fiction, memoirs, humor, poetry and photography. Opinions expressed are those of the authors and do not necessarily reflect the views of the staff, management or publisher of *Chtenia*

Publisher: Paul E. Richardson • Senior Editor: Tamara Eidelman
Contributing Editor: Nina Shevchuk-Murray
Vermont Office Manager: Kate Reilly-Fitzpatrick

Chtenia Subscription rates (1 year): US $35, Outside US $43. All prices are in U.S. dollars. Back issues: when available: $12 (includes shipping and handling in the U.S.). Newsstand: $12 per issue. • To notify us of a change of address, see the subscription address below. To ensure that you do not miss any issues, please notify us 4-6 weeks in advance of any move or address change. Periodical postage paid at Montpelier, VT and at additional mailing offices (USPS 024-769).

Publications Mail Agreement No. 40649170. Return undeliverable Canadian Address to: Station A, PO Box 54, Windsor, ON N9A 6J5. Email: orders@russianlife.com

POSTMASTER: Please send change of address and subscription applications to:
RIS Publications, PO Box 567, Montpelier, VT 05601-0567
orders@russianlife.com
Ph. 802-223-4955 • Fax: 802-223-6105
www.chtenia.com

16

Wisdom & Wit

ЧтениЯReadings
Vol. 4, No. 4 • Fall 2011 • Issue 16

Contents

The Roads to Wisdom

Tamara Eidelman

There is no road Russian Literature has not traversed in pursuit of Wisdom… to obtain insights… to understand something previously unknown, both to the author and to his readers… to witness a Higher Truth shimmering in the sky over Austerlitz, as happened with Prince Andrei in *War and Peace*… to find a teacher like the *starets* Zosima, as did Dostoyevsky's Alyosha Karamazov… to be able to live long enough to grasp why the world is the way it is, and not otherwise… to understand the cause of all sorrows and despair… to know why it is that good fortune only falls to some.

In essence, this is what all of Russian literature is about, though far from all would admit this fact. Some speak openly of their search for Wisdom, while others conceal it behind sad or cynical grins.

Certainly Russian literature has known countless wise men: monks, priests, shamans, holy fools, madmen and just simple fools (or so they appear on first glance). They seek the meaning of life by seeking refuge in the woods, by going to war, by falling in or out of love. And behind it all is the primordial, eternal, "I want to know, why is it so? Why? For whom?"

Of course there are also those who follow false prophets, as pompous and hollow as Kozma Prutkov (page 63) – the fabrication of Alexei Tolstoy and others, who meaningfully intoned: "If you have a fountain, turn it off." Or: "No one can fathom the unfathomable."

And there are those who believe the words of wise men with all their heart and soul, then become disillusioned in them and seek wisdom on the path of simplicity, as did Lev Tolstoy, who renounced his great works and attempted to learn how to live from rural *muzhiks.*

Others, like Balmont (page 38), pronounced:

I've no wisdom that in my poetry I'd share
I seize swift and fleeting moments and place them there

Some, like Vasily Shukshin's hero (*Cutting Them Down to Size*, page 15), believe that wisdom is just a matter of using big words, without regard for their meaning. Still others, like Sergei Dovlatov (*An Officer's Belt*, page 41), follow in the footsteps of Nikolai Gogol, hoping that the road to enlightenment is found by disclosing "through the laughter visible to the world, the tears invisible to it."

So what are we to make of all this? Where does one find the True Path to Wisdom, to an understanding of the Meaning of Life?

Perhaps the greatest wisdom gifted us by Russian literature is the knowledge that there are many such paths, and that every person must decide for themselves which path to follow, and for how long...

The Contributors

KONSTANTIN BALMONT (1867-1942) was a prolific poet and translator of Russia's Silver Age of poetry. Born into a noble family and raised with a love for languages, literature and theater, he had his first poems published at the age of 18. A leading light of the Symbolist movement, he was a tempestuous soul who was repeatedly at odds with the government, first of Tsar Nicholas, then of the Soviets. He and his family left Soviet Russia in 1920, and he lived out the remainder of his life in France.

SERGEI DOVLATOV (1941-1990) was born in Ufa, during his family's evacuation there during WWII. He grew up in St. Petersburg and, while in the army, served as a prison guard. From this sprang his famous novel, *The Zone*. His work was censored from publication in the Soviet Union and he emigrated in 1979. He finally achieved fame in the 1980s, when some of his stories were published in *The New Yorker*.

ZINAIDA GIPPIUS (1869-1945) was a writer, poet and religious thinker, and one of the most influential Russian women of her age. With her husband, Dmitry Merezhkovsky, she founded the Russian Symbolism movement. While she welcomed the February 1917 revolution, she was one of the first artists to publicly denounce the Bolshevik Revolution. She and her husband emigrated to Europe in 1919.

NATALIA KLUCHAROVA was born in Perm and published her first novel, *A Train Named Russia* (2008), online before it was put into print. The book caused a stir in the Russian intelligentsia for its gritty look at modern Russian reality. The novel went on to win Russia's prestigious Debut Prize and has already been translated into eight languages. Her second novel, *Village of Fools*, follows a similar track to her first, exposing in expressive, colloquial prose the eternal questions that have drawn Russian writers since the nineteenth century.

MAYA KUCHERSKAYA is a literary critic, novelist, biographer and teacher. A graduate of Moscow State University, she received a Ph.D from UCLA and is the author of more than 100 articles on literature and culture. She has served several times as a judge on Russia's most prestigious literary award, the Booker, and her first novel (recently rewritten and published as *The Rain God*) received the Student Booker prize. *Faith & Humor: Notes from Muscovy* (published in Russian as *Современный патерик*), from which her contribution to this issue was taken, was shortlisted for the 2006 Bunin Prize and will be published by Russian Life Books in December.

DMITRY MAMIN-SIBIRYAK (1852-1912) was a Russian author best known for his stories and sketches set in the Urals, as well as for his novel *The Privalov Fortune* (1883). The children's story in this issue is one of a series that Mamin-Sibiryak originally wrote for his daughter and later collected as *Tales for Alyona* (*Алёнушкины сказки*, 1894-1896).

KOZMA PRUTKOV (1803-1863) was a literary persona created by Aleksey Tolstoy (the primary contributor), Aleksei, Vladimir and Alexander Zhemchuzhnikov, and Pyotr Yershov. Their creation's supposed works were published in the journals *Sovremennik* ("The Contemporary") and *Iskra* ("The Spark") during the 1850s and 1860s.

YURI RYTKHEU (1930-2008) was born in Uelen, a village in the Chukotka region of Siberia. He sailed the Bering Sea, worked on Arctic geological expeditions, and hunted in Arctic waters, in addition to writing over a dozen novels and collections of stories. His novel *A Dream in Polar Fog* was a Kiriyama Pacific Rim Notable Book in 2006. In the late 1950s, Rytkheu emerged not only as a great literary talent, but as the unique voice of a small national minority – the Chukchi people.

VASILY SHUKSHIN (1929-1974) was the one of most visible and prolific Soviet Russian artists of the sixties and early seventies. He directed five award-winning movies, was a popular and prize-winning actor in over 20 films in just 16 years, and a writer with over 130 short stories, 12 works for stage and screen, and three full-length novels to his credit. The eccentric, soul-searching, and rebellious misfits in his stories, and their metaphysical quandaries, are not only emblematic of his times, but anticipated the themes and protagonists of the writers of the late 1980s, whose work marked the end of Soviet fiction and the rebirth of

Russian literature. Credited with revitalizing the short story as a genre in Russian literature, Shukshin was posthumously honored with the Soviet Union's highest literary prize following his untimely death at the age of forty-five.

IOSIF UTKIN (1903-1944) was a poet and journalist. Born in a remote Siberian outpost, he embraced the Bolshevik revolution early on and worked for many years as a journalist in Irkutsk and then Moscow, while also writing poetry. He fought at the front near Bryansk in World War II and was severely injured. However, he was soon back in the fight, as a journalist and poet-in-residence on the front lines. He died in an airplane crash before the end of the war.

The Translators

ALEXEI BAYER is a New York-based author and translator. He writes in English and in Russian, his native tongue, and translates into both languages. His translations have appeared in *Chtenia* and *Words Without Borders*, as well as in such collections as *The Wall in My Head*, a book dedicated to the 20th anniversary of the fall of the Berlin Wall, and *Life Stories*, a bilingual literary anthology to benefit hospice care in Russia. Original short stories include publications in *New England Review, Chtenia* and *KR Online*. His translation of Maya Kucherskaya's *Faith and Humor: Notes from Muscovy* will be released this fall.

ANTONINA W. BOUIS is one of the most accomplished translators of Russian fiction and nonfiction into English. She has translated a wide variety of authors, from Yevgeny Yevtushenko and Maya Plisetskaya, to Liliya Shevtsova and Edvard Radzinsky. Among her most recent translations are Edvard Radzinsky's *Alexander II: The Last Great Tsar* and Marina Goldovskaya's *Woman with a Movie Camera.*

ILONA YAZHBIN CHAVASS was born in Belarus and emigrated to the United States with her family in 1989. In addition to Yuri Rytkheu, she has translated the work of Dimitry Bortnikov, Sergey Gandlevsky, and Ilya Brazhnikov. Educated at Vassar College, Oxford University and University College London, she now lives in London with her husband and two goldfish.

JOHN GIVENS is associate professor of Russian at University of Rochester, New York, where, he teaches courses on Dostoevsky, Tolstoy and twentieth-century Russian literature and film. He is the author of *Prodigal Son: Vasily Shukshin* *in Soviet Russian Culture* (Northwestern, 2000), the co-translator of *Vasily Shukshin, Stories from a Siberian Village* (Northern Illinois, 1996) and editor (since 1999) of the quarterly translation journal *Russian Studies in Literature*. He is currently writing a book on the image of Jesus Christ in Russian literature.

LAURA GIVENS teaches Russian language at University of Rochester, New York. With John Givens she translated *Vasily Shukshin, Stories from a Siberian Village* (Northern Illinois, 1996), from which the story in this issue was taken. From 1997-2000 she was the translator for *Russian Studies in Literature*, a quarterly journal of translations from the Russian literary press.

JAMIE OLSON teaches in the English Department at Saint Martin's University, just outside of Olympia, Washington. His translations have appeared in *Cardinal Points, Crab Creek Review*, and *Ozone Park Journal*. He writes about poetry, translation, and Russian culture on his site *The Flaxen Wave*.

LYDIA RAZRAN STONE has translated and analyzed biomedical research for NASA, and edits *SlavFile*, the quarterly newsletter for Slavic translators. She has published two books of translated poetry, and has a forthcoming dictionary of English sports idioms. Her translation of Krylov's fairy tales, *The Frogs Who Begged for a Tsar (and 61 other Russia fables by Ivan Krylov)*, was published by Russian Life Books in 2010.

Featured Photographer

YEVGENY MAXIMYUK was born in Kaluga, but now lives in Moscow, where he works in construction. His chief hobbies are photography and motorcycles. Yet he only began to seriously pursue photography in 2008. His favorite genre is the stort of street portraits which are featured in this issue. "My heroes," Yevgeny said, "are average Muscovites." He considers his main achievement in life to be his family – his wife, daughter and granddaughter. To see more of his work, follow the link from this issue on our website.

Street Singer
Yevgeny Maximyuk

Cutting Them Down to Size

Vasily Shukshin

Old Agafya Zhuravlyova's son Konstantin Ivanovich had come home. With his wife and daughter. To have a visit and rest up. Novaya[1] was not a large village, and so when Konstantin Ivanovich actually came rolling up in a taxi, and when everybody in the family took forever dragging suitcase after suitcase out of the trunk, the whole village knew immediately: Agafya's son had come with his family, the middle son Kostya, the rich one, the scholar.

By evening everybody knew all the details: he himself was a Ph.D., his wife was a Ph.D., too, and their daughter was still in school. They'd brought Agafya an electric samovar, a bright flowery robe, and some wooden spoons.

That very evening the *muzhiks* gathered on Gleb Kapustin's porch. They were waiting for Gleb.

At this point, a few words should be said about Gleb Kapustin so that it's clear why the *muzhiks* had gathered on his porch and what they were waiting for.

1. Novaya is Russian for "new."

Gleb Kapustin was a fat-lipped, towheaded *muzhik*, about forty years old, well read, and venomous. Now it had somehow turned out that the village of Novaya, though not large, had produced many notable people: one colonel, two pilots, a physician, and a correspondent... And now there was Zhuravlyov the Ph.D. And somehow it had become the custom that when notable people would come to the village on vacation, when folks would crowd into an *izba* of an evening to see some notable local boy and listen to some wondrous tales or talk about themselves, if the fellow were so inclined – that was the time when Gleb Kapustin would arrive and *cut the table guest down to size*. Many people were displeased with this, but many others, especially the *muzhiks*, just waited for Gleb to come and cut the notable down to size. It wasn't really that they even waited – they'd actually go to Gleb's and then all go see the guest together. Just as if they were going to a performance. Last year Gleb had cut the colonel down to size – brilliantly, beautifully. They'd begun talking about the War of 1812... It became apparent that the colonel didn't know who had ordered the burning of Moscow. That is, he knew that it was some count, but he mixed up the name and said it was Rasputin.[2] Gleb soared high above the colonel like a hawk... and cut him down to size. Everybody got excited, the colonel swore. Some of them ran off to the teacher's house to find out the name of the arsonist count. Gleb Kapustin sat still, flushed in anticipation of the moment of truth, just repeating, "Compose yourself, compose yourself, comrade Colonel. After all, we aren't in Fili, are we?"[3] Gleb emerged the victor while the colonel beat his head with his fist, utterly bewildered. He was very upset. For a long time afterward they talked about Gleb in the village, remembering how he'd just repeated, "Compose yourself, compose

2. The colonel should have said that it was Count Fyodor Rostopchin, the Russian governor and military commander of Moscow, who was alleged to have ordered the burning of the capital in the first days of its occupation by the French, during the War of 1812.
3. Fili (now a suburb of Moscow) was an outlying village where a military council was held on September 1, 1812, at which the Russian commander in chief, General Mikhail Kutuzov, decided to abandon Moscow to the French, rather than risk the Russian army in defending it. Gleb is implying that the question they are debating is not of the same momentous importance as the one discussed in Fili.

yourself, comrade Colonel. After all, we aren't in Fili." They were amazed at Gleb. The old men wondered why he'd put it that way.

Gleb would chuckle and narrow his steely eyes somewhat vindictively. In the village all the mothers of notable people disliked Gleb. They were afraid of him.

And now along came Zhuravlyov the Ph.D.

Gleb came home from work (he worked at the lumberyard), washed up, and changed his clothes. He didn't bother to eat supper. He went right out to join the *muzhiks* on the porch.

They lit up. They talked for a bit about this and that, deliberately avoiding any mention of Zhuravlyov. Then Gleb looked over toward old Agafya Zhuravlyova's *izba* a couple of times, and finally asked:

"Does old Agafya have guests?"

"Ph.D.'s."

"Ph.D.'s?" Gleb was surprised. "O-oh. Won't be able to lick *them* barehanded."

The *muzhiks* laughed. Some folks, they said, couldn't – but some could. And they kept looking impatiently at Gleb.

"Well, let's go and pay a little visit to the Ph.D.'s," Gleb suggested unassumingly.

And so off they went.

Gleb walked a little ahead of the rest, calmly, with his hands in his pockets, squinting at old Agafya's *izba,* where at that moment there were two Ph.D.'s. It generally happened that the *muzhiks* would escort Gleb in this way. It was just like escorting an experienced village fistfighter when folks find out that a new tough guy has appeared in a rival neighborhood.

They didn't talk much on the way.

"What field are the Ph.D.'s in?" Gleb asked.

"What's their specialization? Damned if I know. Old Agafya just told me they were Ph.D.'s. Both him and his wife."

"There are Ph.D.'s in technical fields and then there are those in general studies – they're big on bullshitology."

"All in all, Kostya was a real whiz in math," someone who'd gone to school with Kostya remembered. "He was a straight-A student."

Gleb Kapustin was originally from a neighboring village and didn't know the local notables very well.

"We shall see what we shall see," Gleb promised vaguely. "There are more Ph.D.'s these days than you can shake a stick at."

"He came in a taxi."

"Well, he's gotta maintain his reputation." Gleb gave a short laugh.

Konstantin Ivanovich, Ph.D., greeted his guests cordially and made a fuss about getting some food on the table. The guests waited unassumingly while old Agafya set everything out. They chatted with the doctor and reminisced about how in childhood they had done this or that together.

"Ah, childhood! Those were the days!" the Ph.D. said. "Well, please take a seat at the table, friends."

Everybody sat down at the table. And Gleb Kapustin sat down, too. For the time being Gleb held his tongue. But it was obvious that he was getting ready to pounce. He smiled and went along with their talk about childhood days, but all the while he kept glancing at the Ph.D., sizing him up.

Around the table the conversation got friendlier, they'd even begun to forget about Gleb Kapustin... And then he started in on the doctor.

"What field do you make yourself distinct in?" he asked.

"You mean, where do I work?" The Ph.D. didn't understand.

"Yes."

"The philology department."

"Philosophy?"

"Not exactly... Well, I suppose you could call it that."

"It's a necessary thing." Gleb needed it to be philosophy. He became animated. "Well, and what do you make of primacy?"

"What primacy?" Again, the Ph.D. didn't understand. And he looked attentively at Gleb. Everybody looked at Gleb.

"The primacy of spirit and matter." Gleb threw down the gauntlet. Gleb affected a casual pose and waited for the gauntlet to be taken up. The Ph.D. took the gauntlet up.

"As always," he said with a smile, "matter is primary."

"And the spirit?"

"The spirit comes next, What about it?"

"Is that part of your qualifying exams?" Gleb also smiled. "You'll excuse use. We all… are a long ways away from any centers of learning. Even if a person in these parts wants to have a good chat, it's impossible to round somebody up – there's just nobody to talk to. So, how does philosophy define the concept of weightlessness these days?"

"As it always has. Why 'these days'?"

"It's just that there's this recently discovered phenomenon," Gleb smiled, looking the Ph.D. straight in the eyes. "That's why I'm asking. Natural philosophy, let's suppose, will define it one way, and strategic philosophy quite another."

"But there is no such thing as strategic philosophy," the doctor got all riled up. "What exactly are you talking about?"

"Precisely. But there is a dialectic of nature." Gleb had everybody's attention as he calmly continued. "And philosophy defines nature. Weightlessness has recently been discovered to be one of the elements of nature. That's why I'm asking. Is there a noticeable sense of confusion among the philosophers?"

The Ph.D. broke into sincere laughter. But he was the only one laughing. And he felt awkward. He called his wife over.

"Valya, come here. We're having… the strangest conversation."

Valya came over to the table. But Dr. Konstantin Ivanovich still felt uncomfortable because the *muzhiks* were looking at him, waiting for him to answer the question.

"Let's ascertain," the Ph.D. began seriously, "just what we're talking about."

"All right. Second question. What's your personal opinion about the problem of shamanism in the autonomous regions of the North."

The Ph.D.'s laughed. Gleb Kapustin also smiled. And waited patiently for the doctors to have their laugh.

"Sure, it's possible, of course, to pretend that such a problem doesn't exist. I'll gladly laugh along with you..." Gleb once again smiled magnanimously. He in particular smiled at the doctor's wife, who was also a Ph.D., a Ph.Dame, so to speak. "But even if we do, the problem as such won't just go away. Will it?"

"Are you serious about all this?" Valya asked.

"With your permission." Gleb Kapustin half rose in his seat and bowed with reserve to the Ph.Dame. And he blushed. "The question, of course, is not of global significance, but from the point of view of the likes of us, it'd be interesting to find out."

"Well, what is the question then?" the Ph.D. exclaimed impatiently.

"Your view on the problem of shamanism," Valya prompted, again laughing involuntarily. But she caught herself and said to Gleb, "Sorry."

"That's all right," said Gleb. "I understand that I might have asked a question that's not in your field of specialization."

"But there isn't such a problem!" the doctor blurted out once more, as if delivering a jab straight from the shoulder. This was unfortunate. He shouldn't have done that.

Now it was Gleb who laughed. And he said:

"Well, that makes things easier."

The *muzhiks* looked at the Ph.D.

"Get the woman off the cart and the horse'll go farther," Gleb added, citing a proverb. "There isn't such a problem, and yet these..." (Gleb gestured intricately with his hands) "... natives dance and ring their little bells... Right? But if we want it..." Gleb repeated, "if we w-a-n-t it, it's as if they don't exist. Right? Because if... Very well! One more question. What do you think about the fact that the Moon is a man-made object?"

The Ph.D. looked mutely at Gleb. Gleb continued.

"Scientists have hypothesized that the Moon lies in an artificial orbit and it's assumed that intelligent beings live inside it..."

"Well?" the Ph.D. asked. "What of it?"

"Where are your calculations of the natural trajectories? Where, if at all, can the cosmic sciences be applied?"

The *muzhiks* listened attentively to Gleb.

"If we allow that mankind will be visiting more and more often our, shall we say, cosmic neighbor, we can also assume that one fine moment these intelligent beings will no longer be able to restrain themselves and will crawl out to meet us. Are we ready to understand one another?"

"Who are you asking?"

"You, the thinkers..."

"And are you ready?"

"We aren't thinkers, our salaries aren't that high. But if you're interested, I can share with you in what direction our thoughts are leading us provincials. Let's say an intelligent being has surfaced on the Moon. What would you like us to do? Bark like a dog? Crow like a rooster?"

The *muzhiks* laughed. They stirred in their seats. And once again fixed their eyes attentively on Gleb.

"But, all the same, we need to understand one another. Isn't that right? How?" Gleb paused inquisitively. He looked at everybody. "I suggest drawing a map of our solar system in the sand and showing him that I'm from Earth, you see. And that, even though I'm in a space suit, I also have a head and that I'm an intelligent being, too. To confirm this, it's possible to show him on the map where he's from by pointing at the Moon and then at him. Isn't that logical? And so we've ascertained in this way that we're neighbors. But that's all we've done! Next, I've got to explain the laws by which I've evolved in order to reach my present stage..."

"I see, I see..." The Ph.D. stirred in his seat and shot a meaningful look at his wife. "That's very interesting. Exactly what might those laws be?"

This, too, was unfortunate, because his meaningful look was intercepted. Gleb soared upward... and from way up there in the heavens he swooped down on the Ph.D. And thus it was that in all of the conversations with notable people from the village the moment would arrive when Gleb would soar up like a bird of prey. It was likely that he always looked forward to this moment, exulted in it, because afterward everything else happened automatically.

"Inviting your wife to laugh?" Gleb asked. He asked serenely, but inside he was probably all aquiver. "That's fine... Only, maybe first of all we should at least learn how to read the papers. Huh? What do you think? They say that doesn't hurt Ph.D.'s either..."

"Listen here..."

"No, we've done our listening! We've had, as they say, the pleasure. Therefore, allow me to point out, Mr. Ph.D., that a doctorate is not just a suit, you know, that you buy once and for all. Even so, a suit has to be cleaned sometimes. But a doctorate – that is, if we've agreed that it's not a suit – needs all the more... to be kept up." Gleb spoke quiedy, insistently, without pausing for breath. He was on a roll.

It was uncomfortable to look at the Ph.D. He was clearly at a loss, looking now at his wife, now at Gleb, now at the *muzhiks*. The *muzhiks* tried not to look at him.

"We can be easily impressed around here. All you have to do is roll up to the house in a taxi and drag five suitcases out of the trunk... But you forget that the flow of information moves evenly in all directions. What I mean is that you can also make the wrong impression here. That also happens. You might expect that people around here have never seen Ph.D.'s with their own eyes, but we've seen them, Ph.D.'s and professors and colonels. And we have pleasant memories of them because they are, as a rule, very simple people. So this is my advice to you, comrade Doctor: come down to earth more often. I swear, there's a sound principle behind this. And it's not so risky. It won't hurt so bad when you fall."

"There's a name for this: doing a smear job," said the Ph.D. "What's the matter, did you break loose from your chain? What exactly – "

"I don't know, I don't know," Gleb interrupted him hastily. "I don't know the name for it. I haven't done time nor have I 'broke loose from my chain.' What are you driving at? Around here," Gleb looked at the *muzhiks*, "nobody's done time either – they won't understand you. And your wife here's gaping at you. And your little daughter over there is going to hear you. She'll hear you and she'll 'do a smear job' on somebody in Moscow. So that slang could... end poorly for you, comrade Doctor. Not all means are good, believe me, not all means. After all, when you were taking your qualifying exams, you didn't 'do a smear job' on your professor. Isn't that right?" Gleb rose to his feet. "And you didn't 'use and abuse somebody' to get what you wanted. And you didn't use prison slang. That's because professors are to be respected – your fate depends on them, but it doesn't depend on the likes of us. You can use your prison slang with us. Isn't that how it is? Well, you shouldn't have. We around here also know a thing or two. We also read the papers, and it even happens that we read books from time to time. And we even watch television. And just imagine: we're not in raptures over shows like "The Club of the Jolly and Quick-Witted" or "The Thirteen Chairs Tavern."[4] Why not, you ask? Because it's the very same kind of presumptuousness. That's okay, they say, everybody'll gobble it up. And they do, of course, there's nothing you can do about it. Just don't pretend that all those folks on TV are geniuses. Some of us see right through it. You all should be more modest."

"A typical slandering demagogue," the Ph.D. said, addressing his wife. "All the usual traits are there."

"You're off the mark. I have never, in all my life, written a single denunciation, anonymous or otherwise." Gleb looked at the *muzhiks*: they knew this to be true. "That's not it, comrade Doctor. Do you want me to explain what makes me tick?"

"Please do."

4. The Russian titles are "*Klub veselykh i nakhodchivykh*," a quiz show, and "*Kabachok trinadtsat stulyev*," a sitcom. These two shows enjoyed great popularity throughout the sixties even as they were constantly criticized for their light, diversionary content.

"I like to take people down a peg or two. Don't stick up so high above the waterline. More modesty, dear comrades."

"But where in the world did you see any immodesty in us?" Valya couldn't hold back any longer. "What's so immodest about us?"

"Think good and hard about it when you're all by yourselves. Think it over and you'll understand." Gleb even gave the Ph.D.'s a look of pity. "No matter how many times you say 'honey' it won't make your mouth any sweeter. You don't have to take a Ph.D. exam to understand that. Do you? No matter how many times you write the words 'the people' in all of your articles, nobody's any smarter for it. So when you venture out among those very people, be a little wiser. More prepared perhaps. Or else you may well make a fool of yourself. Goodbye. Have a nice vacation... among the people." Gleb grinned and walked unhurriedly out of the *izba*. He always left alone like that after meetings with notable people.

He didn't hear the *muzhiks* later saying, as they went their separate ways from the Ph.D.s' house:

"Sure did a number on him!... Clever sonuvabitch. How does he know so much about the Moon?"

"Cut him down to size."

"Where does he get it from?"

And the *muzhiks* shook their heads in amazement.

"Clever sonuvabitch. He really put poor Konstantin Ivanych through the wringer... Eh?... Really hung him out to dry. And that Valya, you know, didn't even open her mouth."

"What could you say? Not a damn thing. Kostya, you know, wanted to say something, of course... But he couldn't get a word in edgewise."

"Gotta hand it to him! He's a clever sonuvabitch!"

You could almost even hear a little pity or sympathy for the doctors in the *muzhiks*' voices. Gleb Kapustin, on the other hand, had once again amazed them. He'd astounded them. Even delighted them. But we can't say that they loved it. No, it wasn't a question of loving it. Gleb was cruel, and nobody anywhere has ever yet loved cruelty.

Tomorrow Gleb Kapustin will go to work and ask the *muzhiks* nonchalantly (it's all an act):

"Well, how's that Ph.D. getting on?"

And he'll grin.

"You cut him down to size," they'll tell Gleb.

"No harm done," Gleb will remark magnanimously. "It's good for him. Let him think things over in his spare time. Or else they all get too big for their britches."

First published in Russian: 1970
Translation by Laura and John Givens

Don't Lose Your Head
Yevgeny Maximyuk

Tale of How There Once Was a Fly Who Outlived the Others

Dmitry Mamin-Sibiryak

I

Everyone had so much fun in the summertime! So much! It's hard even to describe everything in the right order... There were so many flies thousands of them. They flew around, buzzed, and enjoyed themselves. When little Baby Fly was born and stretched out her tiny wings, she began to have fun too – so much fun that you can't even describe it. And the most curious thing was that somebody would open all the windows and doors onto the terrace first thing in the morning, so you could fly through whichever one you liked.

"Humans are such kind creatures!" marveled little Baby Fly as she flew from window to window. "These windows were made for us, and they open them up for us too. It's so nice, and more importantly, so fun..."

She flew a thousand times out into the garden, sat on the green grass, and admired it all: the blooming lilacs, the tender little leaves opening on the linden tree, and the flowers in the flowerbeds. The gardener, whom she didn't know yet, had already managed to take care of everything ahead of time. Oh, he was so nice, that gardener! Little Baby Fly hadn't even been born, and he had already managed to prepare absolutely everything she needed. This was all the more amazing because the gardener himself couldn't fly and sometimes even walked only with great effort; he would just stagger along, muttering something incomprehensible.

"And where did all these darn flies come from?" the kind gardener would grumble.

No doubt, the poor man said this purely out of envy, since he could only dig in his garden, plant flowers, and water them – but he couldn't fly. Young Baby Fly purposely flew in circles above the gardener's red nose and pestered him terribly.

Later on, the humans were actually so nice that they would provide all sorts of pleasures just for the flies. For example, in the morning the little girl Alyona would drink milk, eat a roll, and then ask Aunt Olga for sugar – and she did all of this just to leave the flies a few drops of spilt milk and, more importantly, some tidbits of bread and sugar. Well, tell me, what could be more delicious than tidbits like those, especially when you've been flying all morning and have gotten hungry? And the cook Pasha was even nicer than Alyona. Every morning, she would go to the market just for the flies' sake and bring back wonderfully delicious things: beef, sometimes fish, cream, butter – she was simply the nicest woman in the whole house. She knew very well what the flies needed, even though she couldn't fly either, just like the gardener. What a wonderful woman!

And as for Aunt Olga? Oh, that marvelous woman, it seemed, lived her whole life for nobody but the flies... With her own two hands, she would open all the windows each morning to make it easier for the flies to get around, and when it was raining or had become cool outside, she would close them up so that the flies wouldn't get their wings wet or catch cold. Then Aunt Olga noticed that the flies loved sugar and berries, so she took it upon herself to cook berries in sugar every day. Of course, the flies had by now guessed why all of this was done, so they climbed right into the tub of jam out of a sense of gratitude. Alyona also liked jam, but Aunt Olga would only give her one or two spoonfuls so that she wouldn't offend the flies.

Since the flies couldn't eat everything at once, Aunt Olga set aside part of the jam in glass jars (so that it wasn't eaten by mice, who definitely didn't deserve jam). Then she would serve some of it to the flies each day when she drank tea.

"Oh, they're so kind and so good!" young Baby Fly exclaimed, flying from window to window. "It may even be a good thing that humans can't fly. Otherwise, they would turn into flies, big and greedy flies, and they would probably eat up everything themselves... Oh, how nice it is to live in this world!"

"Well, humans aren't quite as kind as you think they are," remarked old Lady Fly, who loved to grumble. "They only seem that way... Have you paid attention to the person they call 'Papa'?"

"Oh, yes... He is a very strange gentleman. You're absolutely right, my dear, kind, old Lady Fly. Why does he smoke his pipe, when he knows very well that I simply can't stand tobacco smoke? It seems to me that he does it just to spite me. And then he doesn't bother to do a single thing for us flies. I once tried a sip of the ink that he's constantly writing something with, and I nearly died... It's simply shocking! I saw with my own eyes how two of the loveliest but completely inexperienced little flies drowned in his inkwell. It was a terrible sight when he fished out one of them with his quill and made a magnificent splotch on his paper... And just imagine, he doesn't blame himself for any of this; no, he blames us! Where is the justice in that?"

"I don't think that this Papa has any sense of justice at all, but he does have one virtue," replied old, experienced Lady Fly. "He drinks beer after lunch. And that's not such a bad habit. I have to admit that I don't mind drinking beer either, even though it makes my head spin... But what can I do? For me, it is a bad habit!"

"I like to drink beer too," admitted young Baby Fly, even blushing a little. "It makes things so fun – so fun! – even though the next day I get a little headache. But maybe Papa doesn't do anything for us flies because he doesn't eat jam, and the only time he eats sugar is when he drops it into a glass of tea. I don't think you can expect anything good from a person who doesn't eat jam. The only thing left for him to do is smoke his pipe."

By and large, the flies knew all the humans well, but they judged each of them quite differently.

II

The summer was hot, and with each passing day more and more flies appeared. They fell into milk, crawled into soup and ink, buzzed, whirled around, and stuck to everything. But our little Baby Fly had already managed to become a truly big Lady Fly and had almost died a few times. The first time, she got her legs so stuck in jam that she could barely climb out; another time, half asleep, she flew onto a lighted lamp and nearly set her wings on fire; the third time, she almost fell between the closing window-frames. All told, she'd had quite enough adventures.

"What is this? Life has become impossible with these flies!" complained Pasha the cook. "It's crazy how they climb everywhere... They need to be exterminated."

Even our own Lady Fly had begun to find that the flies had multiplied too much, especially in the kitchen. In the evenings, the ceiling was covered with what seemed a living, moving net. And when food was brought in, the flies threw themselves onto it in a living heap, shoving each other and arguing nastily. The best pieces were snatched up only by the swiftest and strongest, while the rest got the leftovers: Pasha was right.

But then something horrible happened. One morning, along with the groceries, Pasha brought in a package of some very tasty pieces of paper – that is to say, they became tasty when they were laid out on plates, sprinkled with a little sugar, and doused with warm water.

"Here's a perfect treat for these flies!" said Pasha the cook, setting out the plates in the most visible of places.

Without a word from Pasha, the flies guessed on their own that this had been done for them, and they fell upon the new food in a gleeful mass. Our own Lady Fly dove down onto a plate too, but she was pushed away rather rudely.

"Why are you shoving, ladies and gentlemen?" she said, offended. "Anyway, I wouldn't be so greedy as to take something away from someone else. It's simply impolite..."

After that, the impossible happened. The greediest flies were the first to pay... First, they wandered around like drunkards, and then they collapsed entirely. In the morning, Pasha swept up a whole big plate of dead flies. Only the most sensible ones were left alive, including Lady Fly.

"We don't want those little papers!" everybody squeaked. "We don't want them..."

But the next day the same thing happened again. Out of the sensible flies, only the most sensible survived. But Pasha found that there were too many of even the most sensible ones.

"They make life unbearable..." she complained.

Then, the gentleman they call Papa brought in three very beautiful glass jars, poured some beer into them, and set them on plates. This spelled the end for even the most sensible of the flies. It turned out that the jars were really flytraps. The flies flew toward the smell of beer, ended up in the jar, and died there, unable to find their way out.

"Now that's excellent!" said Pasha approvingly. She turned out to be a completely heartless woman who took pleasure in the misfortune of others.

Judge for yourself: what's so great here? If humans had the same wings as flies, and if you set out a flytrap the size of a house, they would get caught too... Our own Lady Fly, who had learned from the example of even the most sensible flies, stopped trusting humans entirely. They only seem kind, these people, but in reality all they do is spend their whole lives deceiving poor, naïve flies. To tell the truth, humans are the most cunning and evil of all animals!

The fly population had been greatly diminished by all these troubles, but now a new misfortune came along. It turned out that summer had passed, the rains had begun, a cold wind was blowing, and in general unpleasant weather had arrived.

"Is summer really over?" wondered the flies who were left alive. "Tell me, if you will, when did it manage to pass? This is simply unfair… We've hardly had a look around, and now it's autumn already."

This was even worse than the poison papers and glass flytraps. You could seek shelter from the recent nasty weather only with your worst enemy – that is to say, with the humans. But now, the windows weren't opened for days on end, and the skylight was opened only rarely. Even the sun itself seemed to shine only to fool the naïve houseflies. For instance, how do you like this picture? It's morning. The sun is peeping so cheerfully through all the windows that it seems to be inviting all the flies out into the garden. You might start to think that summer has come back again… Well, all right, the naïve flies soar out through the skylight, but the sun only shines on them – it doesn't warm them up. They fly back, but the skylight has been closed. A lot of flies died this way on cold autumn nights, with only their own trustfulness to blame.

"No, you can't trust them," said our own Lady Fly. "I don't trust anything… If even the sun deceives you, then who and what can you trust?"

IT WAS NATURAL that with the arrival of autumn all of the flies underwent an ugly change of mood. Nearly everyone's character was suddenly ruined. There was no trace of their previous joyfulness. They all became gloomy, sluggish, and dissatisfied. Some of them even got to the point where they began to bite, which had never happened before.

Our own Lady Fly's character was so ruined that she didn't recognize herself at all. Earlier, for instance, she had pitied the other flies when they were dying, but now she thought only of herself. She was even ashamed to say out loud what she was thinking: "Well, let them die – there will be more for me."

For one thing, there were very few truly warm corners where a truly decent lady fly could live out the winter, and for another, she was simply fed up with the other flies, who crawled all over everything, snatched the best morsels out from under her nose, and generally behaved rather unceremoniously. It was time for a break.

As if they understood Lady Fly's evil thoughts, the other flies were dying by the hundreds. But as they died, they seemed to be just falling asleep. With each passing day, there were fewer and fewer of them, so there was no need at all for poisoned papers or glass flytraps. Even this wasn't enough for our Lady Fly: she needed to be left completely alone. Just think how delightful it would be: five rooms, and only one fly!

III

And that happy day did finally come. One morning, our Lady Fly woke up rather late. For a long time, she had been feeling uncommonly tired and preferred to sit motionless in her corner under the stove. But now she had the sense that something unusual had happened. She decided to fly towards the window, when everything became suddenly clear. The first snow had fallen. The earth was swaddled in a layer of bright white.

"Ah, so this is what winter looks like!" she grasped immediately. "It's completely white, like a piece of good sugar…"

Then Lady Fly noticed that the other flies had disappeared for good. The poor things hadn't even made it through the first cold snap, falling asleep wherever they happened to be sitting. At another time, Lady Fly would have felt bad for them, but now she thought, "This is excellent… Now I'm all alone! Nobody can eat my jam, my sugar, my crumbs… Oh, how nice!"

She flew through all the rooms and confirmed once more that she was completely alone. Now she could do absolutely anything that she wanted. And how nice that it was so warm in the rooms! Out there on the street it was winter, but in the rooms it was warm and bright and cozy, especially when they would light the lamps and candles in the evening. The first lamp, however, had created a small problem: Lady Fly again flew right onto the flame and almost burnt herself up.

"This must be a winter flytrap," she realized, rubbing her scorched wings. "No, you can't fool me. I understand everything all too well! You want to burn up the last fly, do you? But I'll have none of it... And there's also that stovetop in the kitchen – you think I don't understand that it's a flytrap too?"

The last Lady Fly was happy for a few days, but then she suddenly became bored – so bored, so bored that you can't even describe it. Sure, she was warm, she could eat her fill, but then... Then she began to get bored. She would fly a little, fly some more, take a rest, have a bite to eat, fly a little more – and again she would become more bored than before.

"Oh, I'm so bored," she squeaked in the most pitiful high voice, flying from room to room. "If there were just one little fly left, even a nasty one, but a fly nonetheless..."

No matter how much the last Lady Fly complained about her loneliness, absolutely no one cared enough to understand her. Of course, this irritated her even more, and she went after the humans like a madwoman. She would sit on one person's nose, on another's ear, or else she would start flying back and forth in front of their eyes. In a word, she was a true madwoman.

"My Lord, why don't you people understand that I'm completely alone and dreadfully bored?" she would squeak to each of them. "You can't even fly, so you don't know what boredom is. If somebody would just play with me... But you won't do it! What could be more awkward and clumsy than a human? They're the ugliest beasts that I've ever met..."

Even the dog and cat got tired of the last Lady Fly; everyone was sick of her. And it grieved her more than anything when Aunt Olga said, "Oh, the last fly... Don't touch her, please. Let her live out the winter."

"What is this? It's nothing but an insult," complained Lady Fly. It seemed they had stopped thinking of her as a fly at all. "Sure, 'Let her live' – look what a favor you've done me! And what if I'm bored? And what if, let's say, I don't want to live at all? Well, I don't, so there you have it."

Before that, the last Lady Fly had gotten so angry with everyone that she scared even herself. She flew, buzzed, squeaked... Finally, Spider, who was sitting in a corner, felt bad for her and said, "My dear Lady Fly, come over here... Look how beautiful my web is!"

"Thank you oh so very much... Another friend has turned up! I know all about your beautiful web. You were probably a human once, and now you just pretend to be a spider."

"You know, I only wish you well."

"Oh, how disgusting! Your well wishes mean one thing: you want to eat the last Lady Fly!"

They squabbled fiercely, but still it was boring, so boring, so boring that you can't even describe it. Lady Fly was irritated by absolutely everyone. She grew tired and announced loudly, "If it's going to be this way, if you refuse to understand how bored I am, then I'm going to sit in the corner the whole winter. So there! I'll sit and I won't come out for anything..."

She even began to cry from grief, remembering the joys of the last summer. There had been so many joyful flies, but still she had wanted to be left all alone. That had been a fatal mistake...

Winter stretched on endlessly, and the last Lady Fly began to think that there would never be another summer. She wanted to die, and she cried quietly. It was probably humans who had thought up winter, since they are the ones who think up everything that is harmful to flies. Or had Aunt Olga hidden summer somewhere, just like she hides the sugar and the jam?

The last Lady Fly was ready to die from despair when something extraordinary happened. As usual, she was sitting in her corner and feeling angry when she suddenly heard, "Buzz-zz-zzz!" At first, she didn't believe her own ears and thought that someone was trying to trick her. But then... God, what was that? A real live fly, still quite young, flew past her. The fly had just been born and was happy.

"Spring has begun... Springtime!" she buzzed.

They were so happy to see one another! They hugged, kissed, and even licked each other all over with their little snouts. Old Lady Fly spent a few days describing how nasty the winter had been and how bored she had felt by herself. Young Baby Fly just laughed in a high little voice and simply didn't understand how it could have been boring.

"Springtime! Springtime!" she repeated.

When Aunt Olga allowed the winter window-frames to be taken down and Alyona looked out the first open window, the last Lady Fly immediately understood everything.

"Now I know everything," she buzzed, flying out the window. "Summer is made by us, the flies..."

First published in Russian: 1894-1896
Translation by Jamie L. Olson

Я не знаю мудрости

Константин Бальмонт

Я не знаю мудрости годной для других,
Только мимолетности я влагаю в стих.
В каждой мимолетности вижу я миры,
Полные изменчивой радужной игры.

Не кляните, мудрые. Что вам до меня?
Я ведь только облачко, полное огня.
Я ведь только облачко. Видите: плыву.
И зову мечтателей... Вас я не зову!

I've No Wisdom

Konstantin Balmont

I've no wisdom that in my poetry I'd share;
I seize swift and fleeting moments and place them there.
In each instant, there's a whole world to be seen,
Full of play and motion and iridescent sheen.

Wise men don't you curse me! Why give a thought to me!
Just a cloud, I'm floating. If you look up you'll see.
A fire edged cloud, I grant you, but just passing through.
It's dreamers whom I summon. Why would I call to you?

First published in Russian: 1902
Translation by Lydia Razran Stone

Winter Will Be Here Soon
Yevgeny Maximyuk

This excerpt is one chapter from Sergei Dovlatov's wonderful, semi-autobiographical book, *The Suitcase,* recently republished by Counterpoint. Each chapter in the book gives the back-story for one of the eight items in a long-forgotten suitcase – the only piece of baggage Dovlatov was allowed when he emigrated from the Soviet Union.

An Officer's Belt

Sergei Dovlatov

The worst thing for a drunkard is to wake up in a hospital bed. Before you're fully awake, you mutter, "That's it! I'm through! Forever! Not another drop ever again!"

And suddenly you find a thick gauze bandage around your head. You want to touch it, but your left arm is in a cast. And so on.

This all happened to me in the summer of '63 in the south of the Komi Republic.

I had been drafted a year earlier. I was put in the camp guards, and attended a twenty-day course for supervisors. Even earlier I had boxed for two years. I took part in countrywide competitions. However, I can't recall a single time that the trainer said, "OK. That's it. I'm not worried any more."

But I did hear it from our instructor, Toroptsev, at the prison-supervisor school, after only three weeks. And even though I was going to face recidivist criminals, not boxers.

I tried looking around. Sunspots shone yellow on the linoleum floor. The night table was covered with medicine bottles. A newspaper hung on the wall by the door – *Lenin and Health.*

There was a smell of smoke and, strangely enough, of seaweed. I was in the camp medical unit.

My tightly bandaged head hurt. I could feel a deep wound over my eyebrow. My left arm did not function.

My uniform shirt hung on the back of the bed. There should have been a few cigarettes in there. I used a jar with an inky mixture in it for an ashtray. I had to hold the matchbox in my teeth.

Now I could recall yesterday's events.

I had been crossed off the convoy list in the morning. I went to the sergeant. "What's happened? Am I really getting a day off?"

"Sort of," the sergeant said. "Congratulations… An inmate went crazy in barracks fourteen. Barking, crowing… Bit Auntie Shura, the cook… So you're taking him to the psych ward in Iosser, and then you're free for the rest of the day. Sort of a day off."

"When do I have to go?"

"Now, if you like."

"Alone?"

"Who said anything about alone? Two of you, as required. Take Churilin or Gayenko…"

I found Churilin in the tool shop. He was working with a soldering iron. Something was crackling on the workbench, emanating an odor of rosin.

"I'm doing a bit of welding," Churilin said. "Very fine work, take a look."

I saw the brass buckle with its embossed star. The inside was filled with tin. A belt with a loaded buckle like that was an awesome weapon.

That was the style then – our enforcers all wanted leather officer's belts. They filled the buckle with a layer of tin and went to dances. If there was a fight, the brass buckles flashed over the mêlée.

I said, "Get ready."

"What's up?"

"We're taking a psycho to Iosser. Some inmate flipped out in barracks fourteen. He bit Auntie Shura."

"Good for him," said Churilin. "He obviously wanted some grub. That Shura sneaks butter from the kitchen. I've seen her."

"Let's go," I said.

Churilin cooled the buckle under running water and put on the belt. "Let's roll."

We were issued with weapons and reported to the watch room. About two minutes later the controller brought in a fat, unshaven prisoner. He was resisting and shouting, "I want a pretty girl, an athlete! Give me an athlete! How long am I supposed to wait?"

The controller replied mildly, "A minimum of six years. And that's if you get an early release. After all, you were charged with conspiracy."

The prisoner paid no attention and went on shouting, "Bastards, give me an athletic broad!"

Churilin took a good look at him and poked me with his elbow. "Listen, he's no nut! He's perfectly normal. First he wanted to eat and now he wants a broad. An athlete... A man with taste. I wouldn't mind one, either."

The controller handed me the papers. We went out onto the porch. Churilin asked, "What's your name?"

"Doremifasol," the prisoner replied.

So I said, "If you're really crazy, fine. If you're pretending, that's fine, too. I'm not a doctor. My job is to take you to Iosser. The rest doesn't interest me. The only condition is, don't overplay the part. If you start biting, I'll shoot you. But you can bark and crow as much as you like..."

We had to walk about three miles. There weren't any lumber trucks going our way. Captain Sokolovsky had taken the camp director's car. They said he went off to take some kind of exam. We had to walk on foot.

The road went through a village towards the peat bogs, then past a grove all the way to the highway crossing. Beyond that rose the camp towers of Iosser.

Churilin slowed down near the village store. I handed him two rubles. We didn't have to worry about military police at that hour.

The prisoner was clearly in favor of our idea. He even shared his joy. "My name is Tolik."

Churilin brought back a bottle of Moskovskaya vodka. I stuck it in my jodhpur pocket. We had to hold back until we got to the grove.

The prisoner kept remembering that he was deranged. Then he'd get on all fours and growl. I told him not to waste his strength. Save it for the medical examination. We wouldn't turn him in.

Churilin spread a newspaper on the grass and took a few biscuits from his pocket. We took turns drinking from the bottle. The prisoner hesitated at first. "The doctor might smell it. It would seem unnatural somehow…"

Churilin interrupted. "And barking and crowing is natural?… Have some sorrel afterwards, you'll be fine."

The prisoner said, "You've convinced me."

The day was warm and sunny. Fluffy clouds stretched along the sky. At the highway crossing lumber trucks honked impatiently. A wasp vibrated over Churilin's head.

The vodka was starting to take effect, and I thought, "How good it is to be free! When I get out I'll spend hours walking along the streets. I'll drop by the café on Marata.[1] I'll have a smoke near the Duma building…"

I know that freedom is a philosophical concept. That doesn't interest me. After all, slaves aren't interested in philosophy. To go wherever you want – now that's freedom!

My fellow drinkers were chatting amiably. The prisoner was explaining, "My head isn't working right. And I have gas, too… To tell the truth, people like me should be let out. Written off completely because of illness. After all, obsolete technology is written off, isn't it?"

Churilin interrupted. "Your head isn't working right? You had enough brains to steal, didn't you? Your papers say group theft. What was it you stole, I'd like to know?"

The prisoner was modest. "Nothing much… A tractor."

---

1. Dovlatov was from St. Petersburg, and the reference here are to his haunts in that city.

"A whole tractor?"

"Yeah."

"How did you steal it?"

"Easy. From a reinforced-concrete plant. I used psychology."

"What do you mean?"

"I go in. Get in the tractor. I tie a metal barrel to the tractor and drive to the checkpoint. The barrel's making a racket. The guard comes out. 'Where are you taking that barrel?' And I say, 'It's for personal needs.' 'Got documentation?' 'No.' 'Untie the fucker.' I untie the barrel and drive off. Basically, the psychology worked... And then we took the tractor apart for spare parts."

Churilin slapped the prisoner's back in delight. "You're a real artist, pal!"

The prisoner accepted it modestly. "People admired me."

Churilin suddenly stood up. "Long live the labor reserves!"

He took a second bottle from his pocket.

By then the sun was shining on our meadow. We moved into the shade. We sat down on a fallen alder.

Churilin gave the command, "Let's roll!"

It was hot. The prisoner's shirt was unbuttoned. He had a gunpowder tattoo on his chest that said, "Faina! Do you remember the golden days?!" Next to the words were a skull, a bowie knife and a bottle marked "poison."

Churilin unexpectedly got drunk. I didn't notice it happen. He suddenly grew grim and still.

I knew that the garrison was filled with neurotics. Work as a prison guard inexorably leads to that. But Churilin of all people seemed comparatively normal to me. I remembered only one crazy act on his part. We were taking prisoners out to cut trees. We were sitting around the stove in a wooden shed, keeping warm, talking. Naturally, we were drinking. Churilin went outside without a word, got a pail somewhere, filled it with gasoline, climbed up on the roof and poured the fuel down the chimney. The shed burst into flames. We only just got out. Three people were badly burnt.

But that was a long time ago. So now I said, "Take it easy..."

Churilin silently took out his gun, then barked, "On your feet! The two-man brigade is now under the soldier's command. If necessary, the soldier in charge will use arms. Prisoner Kholodenko, forward march! Private First Class Dovlatov, fall in behind!"

I continued trying to calm him down. "Snap out of it. Pull yourself together. And put away the gun."

The prisoner reacted in camp idiom. "What's the fucking stir?"

Churilin released the safety catch. I walked towards him, repeating, "You've just had too much to drink."

Churilin started backing up. I kept walking towards him, without making any sudden moves. I repeated senseless things out of fear. I remember smiling.

But the prisoner didn't lose spirit. He cried out cheerfully, "Time to run for cover!"

I saw the fallen alder tree behind Churilin. He didn't have far to back up. I crouched. I knew that he might shoot as he fell. And he did.

A bang and a crash of twigs and branches.

The gun fell on the ground. I kicked it aside.

Churilin got up. I wasn't afraid of him then. I could lay him out flat from any position. And the prisoner was there to help.

I saw Churilin take off his belt. I didn't realize what it meant. I thought he was adjusting his shirt.

Theoretically I could have shot him, or at least wounded him. We were on a detail, in a combat situation. I would have been acquitted.

Instead I moved in on him again. My manners got in the way back when I was boxing, too.

As a result Churilin whopped me on the head with his buckle.

Most importantly, I remembered everything. I didn't lose consciousness. I didn't feel the blow itself. I saw blood pouring onto my trousers. So much blood I even cupped my hands to catch it. I stood there and the blood flowed.

Thank goodness, the prisoner didn't lose his nerve. He grabbed the belt away from Churilin. Then he bandaged my head with a shirtsleeve.

Here Churilin began to realize what had happened, I guess. He grabbed his head and headed for the road, weeping.

His pistol lay in the grass, next to the empty bottles. I told the prisoner to pick it up.

And now picture this amazing sight: in front, bawling, is a guard. Behind him, a crazy prisoner with a gun. Bringing up the rear, a private with a bloody bandage on his head. And coming towards them all, a military patrol. A GAZ-61 carrying three men with sub-machine guns and a huge German shepherd.

I'm amazed they didn't shoot my prisoner. They could have shot a round into him easily. Or set the dog on him.

When I saw the car, I passed out. My voluntary reflexes gave way, and the heat took its toll. I just had time to tell them that it wasn't the prisoner's fault. Let them figure out for themselves whose fault it was.

And to top it off, I broke my arm as I fell. Actually, I didn't break it, I damaged it. They found a fracture in the upper arm. I remember thinking that this was really superfluous.

The last thing I remembered was the dog. It sat next to me and yawned nervously, opening its purple jaws.

The speaker over my head began to work – a hum followed by a slight click. I pulled the plug without waiting for the triumphant chords of the national anthem.

I suddenly remembered a forgotten feeling from childhood. I was a schoolboy, I had a fever. I would be allowed to miss school.

I was waiting for the doctor. He would sit on my bed, look at my throat, say, "Well, young man." Mama would look for a clean towel for him.

I was sick, happy, everyone pitied me. I didn't have to wash with cold water.

I was waiting for the doctor. Instead, Churilin showed up. He peeked through the window, sat on the windowsill. Then he stood up and headed towards me. He looked pathetic and beseeching.

I tried to kick him in the balls. Churilin took a step back and, wringing his hands, said, "Serge, forgive me! I was wrong… I repent… Sincerely, I repent! I was in a state of effect – "

"Affect," I corrected.

"All the more so…"

He took a careful step towards me. "I was joking… It was just for a laugh… I have nothing against you…"

"You'd better not."

What could I say to him? What do you say to a guard who uses aftershave only internally?

I said, "What happened to our prisoner?"

"He's fine. Crazy again. Keeps singing 'My Motherland'. He's being tested tomorrow. For the moment, he's in the isolation cell."

"And you?"

"Me? I'm in the guardhouse, of course. That is, actually I'm here, but in theory I'm in the guardhouse. A pal of mine is on duty there… I have to talk to you."

Churilin came another step closer and spoke fast. "Serge, I'm doomed, done for! The comrades' court is on Thursday!"

"For whom?"

"Me. They say I've crippled Serge."

"All right, I'll say I have no charges to bring against you. That I forgive you."

"I already told them you forgive me. They say it doesn't matter, the cup of patience runneth over."

"What else can I do?"

"You're educated, think of something. Put a spin on things. Otherwise those sons of bitches will hand my papers over to the tribunal. That means three years in the disciplinary battalion. And that's even worse than the camps. So you've got to help me..."

He screwed up his face, trying to weep.

"I'm an only son. My brother's doing time, all the sisters are married."

I said, "I don't know what to do. There is one possibility..."

Churilin perked up. "What?"

"At the trial I'll ask you a question. I'll say, 'Churilin, do you have a civilian profession?' You'll reply, 'No.' I'll say, 'What is he supposed to do after his discharge – steal? Where are the promised courses for chauffeurs and bulldozer drivers? Are we any worse than the regular army?' And so on. This will create an uproar, of course. Maybe they'll let you out on bail."

Churilin grew more animated. He sat on my bed and said, "What a brain! Now that's a real brain! With a brain like that there's really no need to work."

"Especially," I noted, "if you whack it with a brass buckle."

"That's in the past," Churilin said, "forgotten... Write down what I'm supposed to say."

"I told you."

"Write it down. Or I'll get mixed up."

Churilin handed me a pencil stub. He tore off a scrap of newspaper. "Write."

I neatly wrote "no".

"What does it mean, 'no'?" he asked.

"You said: 'Write down what I'm supposed to say.' So I wrote: 'No'. I'll ask the question: 'Do you have a civilian profession?' You'll say: 'No.' After that I'll talk about the driving classes. And then the commotion will start."

"So I just say one word, 'no'?"

"Looks that way."

"That's not enough," Churilin said.

"They might ask you other questions."

"Like what?"

"*That* I don't know."

"What will I reply?"

"Depends on what they ask."

"What will they ask? Roughly?"

"Well, maybe: 'Do you admit your guilt, Churilin?'"

"And what will I reply?"

"You reply: 'Yes.'"

"That's all?"

"You could say, 'Yes, of course, I admit it and repent deeply.'"

"That's better. Write it down. First write the question, and then my answer. Write the questions in regular script and print the answers. So I don't confuse them."

Churilin and I worked on this till eleven. The paramedic wanted to chase him out, but Churilin said, "Can't I visit my comrade in arms?"

As a result we wrote an entire drama. We anticipated dozens of questions and answers. And at Churilin's insistence I added parenthetical stage directions: "coldly", "thoughtfully", "bewildered."

Then they brought lunch: a bowl of soup, fried fish and pudding.

Churilin was astonished. "They feed you better here than at the guardhouse."

I said, "I suppose you'd prefer it the other way round?"

I had to give him the pudding and the fish.

After that Churilin left. He said, "My pal at the guardhouse goes off duty at twelve. After that some Ukrainian jerk is on. I have to get back."

Churilin went to the window. Then he returned. "I forgot. Let's trade belts. Otherwise they'll add to my sentence for the buckle."

He took my soldier's belt and hung his on the bed.

"You're in luck," he said. "Mine's real leather. And the buckle is weighted. One blow and a man's out for the count!"

"You don't say..."

Churilin went back to the window. Turned around again. "Thanks," he said. "I won't forget this."

And he climbed out the window. Even though he could easily have used the door.

It's a good thing he didn't take my cigarettes.

Three days passed. The doctor told me I got off easy: all I had was a cut on the head.

I wandered around the military base. Spent hours in the library. Tanned myself on the roof of the woodshed.

Twice I tried to visit the guardhouse. Once a Latvian doing his first year of service was on duty. He raised his sub-machine gun as I approached. I wanted to pass cigarettes through him, but he shook his head.

I dropped by again in the evening. This time, an instructor I knew was on duty.

"Go on in," he said. "You can spend the night if you want."

He rattled the keys. The door opened.

Churilin was playing cards with three other prisoners. A fifth was watching the game with a sandwich in his hand. Orange peels were scattered on the floor.

"Greetings," Churilin said. "Don't bother me. I'm going to flatten them in a minute."

I gave him the cigarettes.

"No booze?" Churilin asked.

One could only admire his gall.

I stood around for a minute and left.

In the morning there were posters all over the place: "Open Komsomol divisional meeting. Comrades' court. Personal case of Churilin, Vadim Tikhonovich. Attendance mandatory."

An old-timer was walking by. "It's about time," he said. "They've gone wild… It's terrible what's going on in the barracks… Wine flowing from under the doors…"

About sixty people were gathered in the club. The Komsomol bureau sat on the stage. Churilin was seated to one side, next to the banner. They were waiting for Major Afanasyev.

Churilin looked absolutely thrilled. Perhaps it was his first time onstage. He gestured, waved to his friends. What's more, he also waved to me.

Major Afanasyev came onstage.

"Comrades!"

Silence gradually came over the hall.

"Comrades! Today we are discussing the personal case of Private Churilin. Private Churilin was sent on an important mission with Private First Class Dovlatov. On the way Private Churilin got as drunk as a skunk and began acting irresponsibly. As a result, Private First Class Dovlatov was wounded, even though he's just as much of a fuckwit, forgive my language… They should have been ashamed of themselves in front of the prisoner at least…"

While the major spoke, Churilin glowed with joy. He patted his hair, twisted in his seat, touched the banner. Clearly, he felt like a hero.

The major went on. "In this quarter alone, Churilin spent twenty-six days in the guardhouse. I'm not talking about drunken behavior – that's like snow in winter for Churilin. I'm talking about more serious crimes, like brawling. You'd think that for him Communism has already been built. He doesn't like your face, he throws a punch! Soon everybody will let fly with their fists. Don't you think *I* get the urge to clock someone in the face? The cup of patience runneth over. We must decide: does Churilin stay with us or do his papers go to the tribunal? It's a serious case, comrades! Let's begin. Tell us how it happened, Churilin."

Everyone looked at Churilin. A crumpled paper appeared in his hands. He turned this way and that, looked it over, and mumbled to himself.

"Speak," Major Afanasyev repeated.

Churilin looked at me in bewilderment. We had not foreseen this. We had left something out of the scenario.

The major raised his voice. "We're waiting!"

"I'm in no rush," Churilin said.

He looked grim. His face was becoming resentful and morose. At the same time the major's voice was growing more irritated. I had to raise my hand. "Let me tell it."

"As you were," the major shouted. "You're a fine one to talk!"

“Aha,” said Churilin. “Here… I want… whatchamacallit… I want to take bulldozer driving courses.”

The major turned to him: “What do courses have to do with it, damn your eyes! You got drunk, maimed your friend, and now you dream about courses!… How about going to college while you’re at it? Or the conservatory?”

Churilin looked at the paper once more and said grimly, “Why are we worse than the regular army?”

The major choked with rage. “How long will this go on? I’m trying to meet him halfway, and this is what he comes out with! I ask him to tell his story and he won’t!”

“What’s there to tell?” Churilin said, jumping up. “*You want some Forsyte Saga* or something? Tell us! Tell us! What’s to tell? What the hell are you bugging me for, you son of a bitch! I can plant one on you, too!”

The major reached for his holster. Red splotches appeared on his cheeks. He was panting. Finally he regained his self-control. “Everything is clear to the court. The meeting is adjourned!”

Two old-timers took Churilin by the arms. I reached for my cigarettes as I headed for the door.

Churilin got a year in the disciplinary battalion. A month before he got out I was discharged. I never saw the crazy prisoner again, either. That whole world disappeared for me.

Only the belt remains.

First published in Russian: 1986
Translation by Antonina W. Bouis

Lime Grove
Yevgeny Maximyuk

Maya Kucherskaya's compelling (and controversial) work of fiction, *Faith and Humor: Notes from Muscovy*, is rich in wisdom, offering a very wry, human look at Russian life and belief. The extracts below are from the first section of the book, which consists of a series of short, instructive (and often puzzling) episodes from the lives of estimable priests and laity. *Faith and Humor* will be published by Russian Life books this December.

Faith & Humor

Maya Kucherskaya

They were all supping around the refectory table. Suddenly, Father Theoprepus got down under the table. He sat there among the monks' roughly shod feet. The feet remained still. Then Father Theoprepus began to move around and to tug at the monks' cassocks from under the table. The monks were humble and no one dared to reproach him. Only one novice asked him in astonishment, "Father, how would you have us interpret this?"

"I want to be like a child," came the answer.

A monk once came to the abbot to complain about another monk.

"He is very bad!" he told the abbot. "Many times I have seen him commit a cardinal sin with my own eyes."

The abbot blindfolded the monk with a filthy, foul-smelling rag and said, "Let us punish the two villains. Let them now see and smell their owner's soul."

"Is my soul really so filthy?" the brother asked.

"Much worse. I actually took pity on you."

From that day forward, whenever the monk saw someone commit a sin, he brought the foul-smelling rag, which he always carried with him, close to his face. And he was comforted.

When he saw a throng of faithful who were waiting for him by his cell, yearning for salvation, Father Paisius took to his heels. The faithful, in their yearning, gave chase, and one of them even caught the priest by the corner of his cassock, but could not hold on to it.

They pursued their recalcitrant spiritual leader for a long time and even trampled two flower beds, but they were quite unable to catch him. They got so upset that they went to complain to the abbot.

The abbot came out onto the porch, gestured to Father Paisius to come over and whispered in his ear, "Why are you running away from your spiritual children, Brother?"

"I am not running away from them," replied the panting Father Paisius. "I am running away from vanity."

An Angel appeared to a monk.

"Are you an Angel?" the monk asked in amazement.

"Yes, I am an Angel," replied the Angel.

"What if you are not a real Angel but only a make-believe one?" the monk asked nervously, making the sign of the cross. "What if you're nothing but a white bird?"

"Whatever do you mean? I am the real thing. If you like, you can touch me."

The Angel stretched out a shining wing.

The monk tried to touch the wing but instead of feathers he felt thin air. Truly it was a real Angel's wing.

The Ascetic

There once was a young man who decided to emulate the church fathers of old. He found some old rusty nails in a shed, fastened them together, fashioning shackles for himself, which caused him horrible pain, scratching his flesh till it bled. Two weeks later, the young man was rushed to the hospital with blood poisoning and it was a miracle he didn't die. Since then he has stopped wearing the shackles and every time he looks at the scars that the nails left on his body he says to himself, "Here, you imbecile, are the fruits of your stupidity."

Father Nicholas loved to read poetry. Whenever he discovered that a visitor was a student of philology, he declared, "Always remember: An I before and an E except after a C."

Some philologists were puzzled by this little statement of his and tried to uncover its secret meaning. Could those letters be the first initials of their friends' names? Or were the letters symbols for Life, Love and the Lord, and the holy man meant that their order could not be changed except by Divine Intervention?

Those were the kinds of thoughts that rushed through philologists' heads, and one of them even noted that sentence down in a notebook and decided to write a learned article about it. But then it dawned on him that it was just a grammar rule, and that someone had invented a simple way to memorize it.

In his previous life, Father Nicholas had been a schoolteacher.

A Humorist

There was once a monk who suffered from depression. He fought against it every way he could, but couldn't beat it. Yet outwardly he seemed to be the happiest man alive. He told jokes and laughed all the time. Only in the final year of his life did he become sad and quiet. He no longer suffered from depression and didn't need to tell jokes. He grew weak and died. During his funeral service the church filled with a sweet odor, so that many thought that lilacs had suddenly begun to bloom. This was because Father Basil had defeated the Devil.

Monks Never Despair

Once, Father Paul had to spend time in the hospital. He had had surgery and it had been unsuccessful. By then, Father Paul was nearly blind. He became despondent. He lay in his room, old, blind and depressed. It was the first time in his life that such a thing had happened to him. He had been tortured and beaten up and starved, but he had never despaired. But now he felt despair gnawing on his soul.

All of a sudden, the doors opened and several men came into his room. They wore mantles and black cassocks.

"Look who is here to visit you," said one of them.

Father Paul raised his head and recognized all the monks whom he had met in jail and in the labor camp, who had been tortured to death or killed and who had been dead for many years. Such were the visitors who came to see him at the local hospital. Father Paul could see them clearly, their faces and every fold of their cassocks.

"Father Paul," one of them said. "It is not meant for a monk to fall into despair."

Then they filed out quietly. As to Father Paul, he immediately regained his spirit and never again despaired.

The Recluse

There was once a priest who began to avoid people, no longer stayed after the service to lead a Bible discussion, didn't visit his flock and stopped taking an interest in their lives. It was as if he could no longer bear it and only wanted them to leave him alone. But people refused to leave him alone. Over the previous 25 years, they had gotten used to seeing him conduct services and they kept calling on him, asking him for guidance and inviting him to visit. Finally, the priest had had enough. He went to the Baikonur Space Center and persuaded the astronauts to make him part of a team training for the next space mission. He was a phenomenally charming man and he could easily make anyone do anything for him. After several months of training, the priest was launched into space along with the others, traveling completely in secret. The spaceship engineers made a special section for him, where he did not stick out so much during live broadcasts from space. This is how the priest got to outer space. He now stares at the blue Earth through the ship's round window, floats in weightlessness, eats, drinks, laughs and implores them to leave him behind to guard the space station, so that he won't have to return to Earth.

Nastya Sakharova, a student at a teacher's college and a faithful devotee of Father Metrophanes, used to say, "When Father Metrophanes gives you his blessing in the morning, you feel for the rest of the day as though you're wearing a fur hat."

"Why a fur hat?" they asked her.

"Because the father's blessing keeps you warm."

Paradise Lost

There once was a priest at a small village church in S–sky Region. His parish was tiny, consisting of ten old ladies and a few vacationers who came during the summer. His wife was his reader and his choir. Rarely did anyone join her in her singing.

The priest's wife was a very sensitive soul, one of those we call "always close to tears." Whenever he conducted a service and came to one of her favorite passages, she began to softly sob. She mourned the Loss of Paradise, and it was at moments such as these that she felt the loss especially keenly. At first she wept softly and continued singing, and that was alright, but as the service went on, her crying got progressively worse. Sometimes she could no longer sing because she was choking back tears. Yet, someone had to continue singing and reading the prayers, loudly and clearly. But how could she continue, when her soul was drowning in tears?

The priest was upset. He had to stop the service, leave the altar and give his reader and singer a stern talking-to, telling her to immediately end this hysteria. But it was to no avail. Or rather, it helped a little, but only for a short while, until his wife again began to think of the Loss of Paradise. It was lost and gone for good.

One day, the priest's patience ran out. He came out from behind the altar and gave his wife a slap to the head. Then another one, and then a third.

And what do you think happened next?

The priest's wife didn't take offense, but from that day forward learned to weep silently. She kept her tears to herself, so that no one could see them. She still wept, but the service went on as usual. It was a steady and dignified service. The priest was very happy, because there were no more interruptions or distractions due to her sobbing. The faithful prayed, lit candles and kissed the icons. Everything was fine.

There was just one thing wrong: the Paradise was now truly lost.

A Chance Meeting

Father James Potter didn't believe in miracles. Whenever he heard about an icon shedding tears or a person having a vision, or about a prophetic dream or the hearing of voices, he grimaced and sighed, "Guys, let's be reasonable now."

Whenever the conversation touched upon holy men or, worse, seers, he promptly got up and left the room.

Not long before he died, he had a visitation. He was visited by a woman dressed in white, pale and wearing a plain, long canvas dress. Father James was quite ill by then and could barely get out of bed. The woman stood at the head of his bed. She had come in unexpectedly, simply materializing out of the wall. Her hand passed through the wooden headboard and Father James concluded that she was not of flesh and blood. The priest pushed a chair against his visitor but she didn't even move. He managed to gather up enough strength to ask her, "You want me to believe that you're not a hallucination? You want me to believe that you're a miracle?"

"No," said the woman simply. "I'm not a miracle. I'm death."

First published in Russian: 2005
Translation by Alexei Bayer

Portrait of Kuzma Prutkov
Lev Zhemchuzhnikov, Alexander Beyderman and Lev Lagorio

Kozma Prutkov's satirical poems and aphorisms and the description of his persona (page 65) ridiculed the mental stagnation and political correctness of his age and parodied second-rate, derivative literary figures. Some of Prutkov's maxims are non-sensical, others are profound, and many (of both stripes) have entered the Russian lexicon as "winged phrases." For this reason, this selection is presented bilingually.

Uncommon Wisdom

Kozma Prutkov[1]

Обручальное кольцо есть первое звено в цепи супружеской жизни.

The wedding ring is the first link in the chain of married life.

Никто не обнимет необъятного.

No one can fathom the unfathomable.

Смотри в корень!

Get to the root of the matter!

Слабеющая память подобна потухающему светильнику.

A failing memory is like a guttering oil lamp.

Слабеющую память можно также сравнивать с увядающею незабудкою.

A failing memory may also be likened to a fading forget-me-not.

Слабеющие глаза всегда уподоблю старому потускневшему зеркалу, даже надтреснутому.

I would compare failing eyesight to an old mirror that has lost its luster, and even to one that is cracked.

---

1. Kozma Petrovich Prutkov was a literary persona created by Aleksey Tolstoy (the primary contributor), the Brothers Zhemchuzhnikov, and Pyotr Yershov. Their creation's supposed works were published in the journals *Sovremennik* ("The Contemporary") and *Iskra* ("The Spark") during the 1850s and 1860s.

Воображение поэта, удрученного горем, подобно ноге, заключенной в новый сапог.

When a poet's imagination is dulled by sorrow, it becomes like a foot pinched by a new boot.

Если хочешь быть красивым, поступи в гусары.

If you dream of being handsome, join the Hussars.

Человек, не будучи одеян благодетельною природою, получил свыше дар портного искусства.

To man, left naked by benevolent nature, Providence gave the gift of tailoring.

Полезнее пройти путь жизни, чем всю вселенную.

It is more profitable to walk the road of life from end to end than to traverse the entire universe.

Если у тебя есть фонтан, заткни его; дай отдохнуть и фонтану.

If you have a fountain, turn it off. Even a fountain deserves a rest.

Усердный врач подобен пеликану.

A hard-working doctor is like a pelican.

Умные речи подобны строкам, напечатанным курсивом.

Wise words are like lines printed in italics.

Смерть для того поставлена в конце жизни, чтобы удобнее к ней приготовиться.

Death was wisely placed at the end of life so we would have time to prepare for it.

Ничего не доводи до крайности: человек, желающий трапезовать слишком поздно, рискует трапезовать на другой день поутру.

Do not take anything to extremes: a man attempting to sup as late as possible risks eating supper on the morning of the next day.

Вытапливай воск, но сохраняй мёд.

Discard the wax, but keep the honey.

Пояснительные выражения объясняют тёмные мысли.

Elucidations cast light on dark thoughts.

Biographic Details of Kozma Prutkov

Kozma Petrovich Prutkov spent his whole life, aside from his childhood and early adolescence, in government service: first in the military and then in the civil service. He was born on April 11, 1803, in the village of Tenteleva near Solvychegodsk, and died on January 13, 1863.

He owned an estate in the hamlet of Pystynok near the Sablino railroad station.

In 1820 he entered military service, solely in order to be able to wear a uniform, but spent only two and a half years in the Hussars. On the night of April 10-11, 1823, he returned home late after getting drunk with his comrades. He had just gotten into bed when, right before his eyes, there appeared a naked brigadier general, who seized his hand and pulled him from his cot. Without giving Prutkov time to dress, the general led him in silence along a kind of long, dark corridor to the top of a high mountain peak. There he began to remove various precious materials from an ancient crypt, showing them to Prutkov one by one, even draping some of them over his trembling body. Prutkov waited in confusion and terror for the upshot of this incomprehensible event, but, suddenly, just as the most precious material of all touched him, he felt a strong electric shock throughout his body and awoke bathed in sweat. It is not known exactly what significance Kozma Prutkov attributed to this vision. However, he described it frequently afterwards, always with a great deal of emotion, concluding his tale with the loud announcement, "The next morning, the moment I woke up, I decided to leave my regiment, resigned my commission and, when my resignation came through, I immediately found a position serving in the Ministry of Finance in the Assay Bureau, where I intend to remain for the rest of my life!" Indeed, after joining the Assay Bureau, he remained there until his death, that is until January 13, 1863.

His superiors at the Ministry singled him out for praise, promotion and decoration. In this Bureau he succeeded in climbing all the rungs of the civil service ladder, up to and including the rank of Actual State Councilor and attaining the highest position in the Bureau, that of its director. Subsequently, he was decorated with the Order of St. Stanislav, 1st degree, which gratified him greatly, as can be seen in the fable *Star on the Belly*.

In general, he was very pleased with his career. But there was one period, when major reforms were being planned under the previous tsar [Alexander II], that he seemed to lose his composure. At first he felt as if the rug was being pulled out from under him, and he starting complaining, shouting everywhere about the prematurity of all reforms and about how he himself was "an enemy of all such so-called issues!"

However, when, later, it became clear that reforms were unavoidable, he tried to distinguish himself by coming up with his own reform projects and reacted with extreme indignation when his projects were rejected on the grounds of their obvious lack of merit. He attributed these rejections to envy and lack of respect for his experience and years of service and began to fall into states of depression, and even despair. In one of his moments of black despair he wrote the mystery play *All Wordly Powers are Akin*.

Soon, however, he calmed down, and began to sense that in actuality nothing had changed: the same atmosphere still surrounded him and the same ground remained beneath his feet. He again began to propose projects, but this time they were repressive in nature and were accepted and approved. This allowed him to return to his previous level of self-satisfaction and to expect still further service promotions. The sudden stroke that felled him in the director's office of the Assay Bureau put an end to such hopes and to his days of glory.

– January 13, 1884

Не всякому человеку даже гусарский мундир к лицу.

Even a hussar's uniform is not becoming to everyone.

Бди!

Watch out!

Никто не обнимет необъятного.

No one can fathom the unfathomable.

Три дела, однажды начавши, трудно кончить: а) вкушать хорошую пищу; б) беседовать с возвратившимся из похода другом и в) чесать, где чешется.

There are three activities that are hard to stop once you have begun: a) eating good food; b) chatting with a friend who has just come back from a trip; and c) scratching an itch.

Достаток распутного равняется короткому одеялу: натянешь его к носу, обнажатся ноги.

The fortune of a profligate man is like a blanket that is too short. When you pull it up to your chin for warmth, you uncover your feet.

Не растравляй раны ближнего; страдающему предлагай бальзам... Копая другому яму, сам в нее попадешь.

Do not rub salt into other people's wounds, but instead offer them balm. If you dig a pit for someone else, you are likely to fall in it yourself.

Если у тебя спрошено будет: что полезнее, солнце или месяц? – ответствуй: месяц. Ибо солнце светит днём, когда и без того светло; а месяц – ночью.

If people ask you whether the sun or the moon is more useful, answer that it is the moon. After all, the sun only shines during the day, when it is already light. The moon, however, provides needed light in the night's darkness.

Но, с другой стороны: солнце лучше тем, что светит и греет; а месяц только светит, и то лишь в лунную ночь!

On the other hand, the sun might be considered better because it both shines and warms, while all the moon does is shine and then only on nights that are moonlit!

Рассуждай токмо о том, о чём понятия твои тебе сие дозволяют. Так: не зная законов языка ирокезского, можешь ли ты делать такое суждение по сему предмету, которое не было бы неосновательно и глупо?

Do not make pronouncements about things you know nothing about. For example, if you do not know the grammar of the Iroquois language, anything you try to say about it is sure to be not only wrong but stupid.

Щёлкни кобылу в нос – она махнет хвостом.

If you flick a mare on the nose, she will swish her tail.

Не робей перед врагом: лютейший враг человека – он сам.

Do not fear the enemy: man's worst enemy is man himself.

И терпентин на что-нибудь полезен!

Even turpentine is good for something!

Всякий необходимо причиняет пользу, употреблённый на своём месте. Напротив того: упражнения лучшего танцмейстера в химии неуместны; советы опытного астронома в танцах глупы.

Anyone employed in his proper place will not fail to be of use. On the contrary, it would be inappropriate for even the finest dancing master to perform chemical experiments, while pointers on how to dance offered by even the most learned astronomer would be stupid.

Говорят, что труд убивает время; но сие последнее, нисколько от этого не уменьшаяся, продолжает служить человечеству и всей вселенной постоянно в одинаковой полноте и непрерывности.

It is said that work kills time. However, it is not true that labor diminishes time even slightly. Time continues to serve humanity and the entire universe with unwavering completeness and continuity.

На дне каждого сердца есть осадок.

At the bottom of every person's heart you will find sediment.

Под сладкими выражениями таятся мысли коварные: так, от курящего табак нередко пахнет духами.

Treacherous thoughts are concealed beneath sweet words in the same way that a smoker often smells of cologne.

Многие вещи нам непонятны не потому, что наши понятия слабы; но потому, что сии вещи не входят в круг наших понятий.

We are unable to understand certain things not because our understanding is weak, but because the things themselves are beyond the range of our understanding.

Никто не обнимет необъятного!

No one can fathom the unfathomable!

Ногти и волосы даны человеку для того, чтобы доставить ему постоянное, но лёгкое занятие.

Men have been given fingernails and hair to provide them with an occupation that is constant but not onerous.

Жизнь – альбом. Человек – карандаш. Дела – ландшафт. Время – гумиэластик: и отскакивает и стирает.

Life is an album. Man is a pencil. Deeds are a landscape. Time is an eraser that bounces in and erases everything.

Смотри вдаль – увидишь даль; смотри в небо – увидишь небо; взглянув в маленькое зеркальце, увидишь только себя.

Look into the distance and you will see the distance; look into the sky and you will see the sky; but if you look into a little mirror, all you will see is yourself.

Где начало того конца, которым оканчивается начало?

Where is the beginning of that end that puts an end to the beginning?

Чем скорее проедешь, тем скорее приедешь.

The faster you go, the sooner you will arrive.

Если хочешь быть счастливым, будь им.

If you want to be happy, then be happy.

Петух пробуждается рано; но злодей ещё раньше.

The rooster wakes early, but evildoers – even earlier.

И устрица имеет врагов!

Even an oyster has enemies!

Не шути с женщинами: эти шутки глупы и неприличны.

Do not joke with women. Such jokes are stupid and improper.

Чрезмерный богач, не помогающий бедным, подобен здоровенной кормилице, сосущей с аппетитом собственную грудь у колыбели голодающего дитяти.

An excessively rich man who does not help the poor is like a healthy wet nurse who drinks heartily from her own breast at the cradle of a starving baby.

Человек раздвоен снизу, а не сверху, – для того, что две опоры надёжнее одной.

Man is cloven below and not above – because two supporting structures are more reliable than one.

Глупейший человек был тот, который изобрёл кисточки для украшения и золотые гвоздики на мебели.

The man who invented decorative fringe and gilded studs for adorning furniture has to be the stupidest person in the world.

Многие люди подобны колбасам: чем их начинят, то и носят в себе.

Many people are like sausages: whatever someone stuffs them with, that is what they have inside them.

Специалист подобен флюсу: полнота его одностороння.

A specialist is like a cheek swollen with a toothache – it is full on only one side.

Взирая на высоких людей и на высокие предметы, придерживай картуз свой за козырёк.

When you gaze at exalted people and exalted objects, hold on to your cap.

Плюнь тому в глаза, кто скажет, что можно обнять необъятное!

Spit in the eye of anyone who says that it is possible to fathom the unfathomable.

Если на клетке слона прочтёшь надпись “буйвол”, не верь глазам своим.

If you read a sign that says “buffalo” on a cage containing an elephant, do not believe your eyes.

Муравьиные яйца более породившей их твари; так и слава даровитого человека далеко продолжительнее собственной его жизни.

The eggs of ants are larger than the creatures themselves. In the same way, the fame of a talented man lasts far longer than his own life.

Глядя на мир, нельзя не удивляться!

It is impossible to gaze at the world and not be amazed!

Самый отдалённый пункт земного шара к чему-нибудь да близок, а самый близкий от чего-нибудь да отдалён.

The most remote point on the earth is close to something, and the closest point is remote from something else.

Философ легко торжествует над будущею и минувшею скорбями, но он же легко побеждается настоящею.

A philosopher easily triumphs over future and past sorrows, but he is equally easily conquered by one in the present.

Небо, усеянное звёздами, всегда уподоблю груди заслуженного генерала.

The sky sprinkled with stars is like the chest of a much-decorated general.

Доблий муж подобен мавзолею.

A valiant man is like a mausoleum.

Человеку даны две руки на тот конец, дабы он, принимая левою, раздавал правою.

Man has been given two hands so that what he receives with the left he can give away with the right

Ревнивый муж подобен турку.

A jealous husband is like a mule.

Вестовщик решету подобен.

A gossip is like a sieve.

Всегда держись начеку!

Always be on the lookout!

Спокойствие многих было бы надёжнее, если бы дозволено было относить все неприятности на казённый счёт.

Many people would have more peace of mind if they were permitted to charge all their troubles to the government account.

Не ходи по косогору, сапоги стопчешь!

Do not walk on a hillside, you will wear out your boots!

Советую каждому: даже не в особенно сырую и ветреную погоду закладывать уши хлопчатою бумагою или морским канатом.

I advise everyone to stuff their ears with cotton or nautical rope, even in weather that is not especially damp or windy.

Кто мешает тебе выдумать порох непромокаемый?

Who is stopping you from inventing waterproof gunpowder?

Снег считают саваном омертвевшей природы; но он же служит первопутьем для жизненных припасов. Так разгадайте же природу!

Snow is called the shroud of dead nature, but only snow makes it possible to deliver vital supplies in the winter. Don't second-guess Nature!

Барометр в земледельческом хозяйстве может быть с большою выгодою заменён усердною прислугою, страдающею нарочитыми ревматизмами.

It would be economical to replace the barometers used in agriculture with a diligent servant who claims to suffer from rheumatism.

Собака, сидящая на сене, вредна. Курица, сидящая на яйцах, полезна. От сидячей жизни тучнеют: так, всякий меняло жирен.

A dog sitting on a haystack is harmful. A chicken sitting on eggs is beneficial. The sedentary life makes people gain weight, which is why all moneychangers are fat.

Всякая человеческая голова подобна желудку: одна переваривает входящую в оную пищу, а другая от неё засоряется.

Every man's head is like a stomach: one person's head digests the food that enters it, while another's just gets clogged up.

И при железных дорогах лучше сохранять двуколку.
Even now that we have railroads, it would not be advisable to get rid of your two-wheeled cart.

Если бы всё прошедшее было настоящим, а настоящее продолжало существовать наряду с будущим, кто был бы в силах разобрать: где причины и где последствия?
If all the past were the present, and the present continued to exist along with the future, who would be able to tell what were causes and what were effects?

Счастье подобно шару, который подкатывается: сегодня под одного, завтра под другого, послезавтра под третьего, потом под четвёртого, пятого и т.д., соответственно числу и очереди счастливых людей.
Happiness is like a ball that rolls over to one person today, and over to another tomorrow, the day after to a third, then to a fourth and fifth, etc., according to the number and sequence of happy people.

Не совсем понимаю: почему многие называют судьбу индейкою, а не какою-либо другою, более на судьбу похожею птицею?
I fail to understand why many people liken fate to a turkey. Instead, they should compare it to some other bird bearing a greater resemblance to fate.

Козыряй!
Play your trump card!

Издание некоторых газет, журналов и даже книг может приносить выгоду.
The publication of a few newspapers, journals, and even books, may be profitable.

Бросая в воду камешки, смотри на круги, ими образуемые; иначе такое бросание будет пустою забавою.
When you throw pebbles into the water, observe the ripples they form. Otherwise you will have wasted your time.

Опять скажу: никто не обнимет необъятного!
Once again I remind you: it is not possible to fathom the unfathomable.

Вред или польза действия обуславливается совокупностью обстоятельств.

The harmfulness or benefit of an action is the consequence of a combination of circumstances under which it is undertaken.

Ветер есть дыхание природы.

Wind is nature's way of breathing.

Смерть и солнце не могут пристально взирать друг на друга.

Death and the sun cannot bear to look each other straight in the eye.

Сократ справедливо называет бегущего воина трусом.

Socrates was correct when he called the fleeing warrior a coward.

Весьма остроумно замечает Фейербах, что взоры беспутного сапожника следят за штопором, а не за шилом, отчего и происходят мозоли.

How very wise was Feuerbach's observation that the eyes of the dissolute shoemaker are focused on his corkscrew rather than his awl, which explains the existence of blisters in the world.

Друзья мои! идите твёрдыми шагами по стезе, ведущей в храм согласия, а встречаемые на пути препоны преодолевайте с мужественною кротостью льва.

My friends! Stride confidently along the road leading to the temple of accord, and overcome the obstacles on your path with the manly meekness of a lion.

Правда не вышла бы из колодезя, если бы сырость не испортила её зеркала.

Truth would not have left the well, if the dampness had not fogged her mirror.

Век живи – век учись! и ты наконец достигнешь того, что, подобно мудрецу, будешь иметь право сказать, что ничего не знаешь.

Live and learn! And ultimately, like the sage, you will gain the right to say that you know nothing.

Сребролюбцы! сколь ничтожны ваши стяжания, коли все ваши сокровища не стоят одного листка из лаврового венка поэта!

Worshippers of Mammon! How meaningless are your pitiful efforts to acquire wealth. when your entire treasure hoard is not worth a single leaf from a poet's laurel wreath!

Человек довольствует вожделения свои на обоих краях земного круга!

Mankind exercises lechery on both hemispheres of the globe.

Не уступай малодушно всеобщим желаниям, если они противны твоим собственным; но лучше, хваля оные притворно и нарочно оттягивая время, норови надуть своих противников.

Do not, like a coward, go along with the desires of the majority when they are counter to your own. Rather, pretend to praise them and by wasting their time attempt to bamboozle your opponents.

Чиновник умирает, и ордена его остаются на лице земли.

The civil servant dies but the service medals he was awarded remain on the face of the Earth.

Не всякий генерал от природы полный.

Not all generals are naturally stout.

Отнюдь не принимай почетных гостей в разорванном халате!

Never receive honored guests in a tattered robe!

Бывает, что усердие превозмогает и рассудок

It may happen that hard work overcomes even reason.

Незрелый ананас, для человека справедливого, всегда хуже зрелой смородины

To a wise man, an unripe pineapple is always less desirable than a ripe currant.

Одного яйца два раза не высидишь!

You cannot hatch the same egg twice!

Пробка шампанского, с шумом взлетевшая и столь же мгновенно ниспадающая, – вот изрядная картина любви.

A champagne cork that flies out with a bang and then immediately drops to the ground: what a perfect metaphor for love.

Стоящие часы не всегда испорчены, а иногда они только остановлены; и добрый прохожий не преминет в стенных покачнуть маятник, а карманные завести.

Even if a timepiece has stopped, this doesn't always mean it is broken. Sometimes it has merely run down and a virtuous passer-by should not pass up the opportunity to restart the pendulum of a wall clock or wind a pocket watch.

Лжёт непростительно, кто уверяет, будто всё на свете справедливо! Так, изобретший употребление сандарака может быть вполне убеждён, что имя его останется неизвестно потомству!

Anyone who says that there is always justice in the world is a terrible liar! For example, the man who discovered a use for sandarac resin may be sure that his name will remain unknown to posterity.

Даже летом, отправляясь в вояж, бери с собой что-либо тёплое, ибо можешь ли ты знать, что случится в атмосфере?

When you set out on a journey, be sure to take something warm with you, even in summer! Who knows what the weather might get up to?

Иногда слова, напечатанные курсивом, много несправедливее тех, которые напечатаны прямым шрифтом.

Sometimes words printed in italics are much more unjust than those printed in ordinary type.

Не всякому офицеру мундир к лицу.

Not all officers look good in their uniforms.

Трудись как муравей, если хочешь быть уподоблен пчеле.

Work like an ant if you wish to emulate the bee.

Мудрость, подобно черепаховому супу, не всякому доступна.

Like turtle soup, wisdom is not available to everyone.

Знай, читатель, что мудрость уменьшает жалобы, а не страдания!

Reader, be aware that wisdom lessens complaints, not suffering!

Дружба согревает душу, платье – тело, а солнце и печка – воздух.
Friendship warms the heart, clothing the body, while the sun and stoves warm the air.

И мудрый Вольтер сомневался в ядовитости кофе!
Even Voltaire doubted that coffee is poisonous.

Настоящее есть следствие прошедшего, а потому непрестанно обращай взор свой на зады, чем сбережёшь себя от знатных ошибок.
The present arises as a consequence of the past, so always keep your eye on your posterior in order to keep yourself from making serious mistakes.

Не печалуйся в скорбях, – уныние само наводит скорби.
Do not let afflictions grieve you; depression in itself brings on afflictions.

Не прибегай к щекотке, желая развеселить знакомую, – иная назовёт тебя за это невежей.
Even if you want to cheer up a lady of your acquaintance, it is not a good idea to tickle her – she may consider this impolite.

Говоря с хитрецом, взвешивай ответ свой.
When you are talking with a sly fellow, choose your words carefully.

Не во всякой игре тузы выигрывают!
Aces do not win every game.

Купи прежде картину, а после рамку!
Buy the painting first and only then the frame.

От малых причин бывают весьма важные последствия; так, отгрызение заусенца причинило моему знакомому рак.
Small things can have extremely significant consequences. Thus someone I know got cancer from biting off a hangnail.

Ценность всего условна: зубочистка в бисерном чехле, подаренная тебе в сувенир, несравненно дороже двух рублей с полтиной.
Everything's worth is relative. For example a toothpick in a beaded case, given to you as a memento, is worth incomparably more than two and a half rubles cash.

Почти всякое морщинистое лицо смело уподоблю груше, вынутой из компота.
Virtually every wrinkled face is like a stewed pear.

И египтяне были в своё время справедливы и человеколюбивы!
In their day, even the Egyptians were just and humane!

Есть ли на свете человек, который мог бы обнять необъятное?
Is there a single man on earth who would be able to fathom the unfathomable?

Отыщи всему начало, и ты многое поймешь.
Seek the principle underlying everything and you will understand a great deal.

Новые сапоги всегда жмут
New shoes always pinch.

Когда народы между собою дерутся, это называется войною.
When nations squabble among themselves, it is called war.

First published in Russian: 1850s-1860s
Translation by Lydia Razran Stone

Мудрость

Иосиф Уткин

Когда утрачивают пышность кудри
И срок придет вздохнуть наедине,
В неторопливой тишине
К нам медленно подходит мудрость.

Издалека. Спокойствием блистая
(Будильник скуп! Будильник слаб!),
Как к пристани направленный корабль,
Она величественно вырастает...

Но вот пришла. И многое – на убыль:
Непостоянство, ветреность, порыв...
И перламутровый разлив
Уж редко открывает губы.

И пусть потом нам девушка приснится,
Пусть женщина перерезает путь,–
Мы поглядим не на тугую грудь,
Мы строго взглянем под ресницы.

И пусть – война. Воинственным азартом
Не вспыхнем, нет, и сабли не возьмем.
Есть умный штаб. Есть штаб, и в нем
Мы прокорпим над паутиной карты.

И ждем побед,
Но в том же мерном круге
(Победы ждем без ревностей глухих)
Не как лукавую любовницу – жених,
Как муж – степенную и верную супругу.

Wisdom

Joseph Utkin

When they are sparse, the curls that frame our face,
And sighing we must face old age alone,
Then in the silence of the dawn
To us comes wisdom with unhurried pace.

From far away she comes, serene and glowing.
(Though nothing we can do can speed the clock!)
A stately ship arriving at her dock
And, as we watch we see her outline growing.

She's here at last. And now so much subsides –
Frivolity, inconstancy, caprice...
Those pearly floods of impulse nearly cease,
As we let sense and wisdom be our guides.

And if some lovely woman comes our way
Or dreams of beauties interrupt our rest
We do not turn to gaze upon her breast,
But sternly, in our wisdom, turn away.

And if a war should come, we'll still not lapse
Into a state of passion, yearn to fight.
Instead we'll seek a staff job where we might
Best serve the cause perusing dusty maps.

And patiently for victory we'll wait
(Quite confident that it will come to pass);
Not like a suitor for some flightly lass,
But like a husband for a true and faithful mate.

First published in Russian: 1925
Translation by Lydia Razran Stone

At Church
Yevgeny Maximyuk

This selection is from Rytkheu's book, *The Chukchi Bible,* a collection of the myths and stories of Rytkheu's own family that is at once a moving history of the Chukchi people and a beautiful cautionary tale rife with conflict, human drama, and humor. The book was published this year by Archipelago Books.

The School for Shamans

Yuri Rytkheu

The inside of Kalyantagrau's *yaranga* was always permeated by a faint but potent odor, though there was nothing out of the ordinary there, nothing different from the contents of any other *yaranga* in Uelen. To the right of the entrance, behind two wooden barrels where stores of walrus blubber and pickled greens were kept, towered a voluminous chest for fur-lined clothing and deerskins; behind the chest were more barrels. To the left was the firepit, clad in a casing of flat thin stones, all of them blackened with soot; a similarly greasy and blackened iron chain, hooked at the end, was rigged to be lowered into the fire from above. Beyond the fire pit, more barrels and household implements. The wooden supporting walls were hung with hunting gear. The necessary kit for seal hunting was composed of an *akyn* – a wooden toggle hooked on the end of a rope used to retrieve a kill from the water – a spool of thin nerpa-skin string, bone hooks, buttons, and a small bag whose contents were as yet unknown to Mletkin. Next to it, were two pairs of "raven claws" – snowshoes fashioned from wooden frames netted over with lakhtak-hide thongs – and two matching walking staffs, one with a sharp hook at one end and a long metal spike on the other, used to sound the thickness of new ice. The second staff was the usual kind, for leaning on as one walked. There were storerooms along each side of the *polog*, too. Maybe that was where the shaman kept the objects he used in his rituals, the tambourines and holy vessels... There was not an idol in sight, though in any other Uelen *yaranga* the Keeper of the Home would be easy to spot.

In addition to its master and his wife, Minu, their daughter Itchel' and son Vukvun also lived in the *yaranga*. Both were older than Mletkin and he regarded them as adults. Itchel', a stringy, sickly young woman, had some sort of an emotional distemper. Abruptly, she would go rigid and stare into space with unseeing eyes, as though absenting herself from the world. She could remain in this suspended state for hours. The whole village knew about the young woman's peculiarity and left her alone during her spells. Eventually she would come to and resume her interrupted task or conversation as though the pause had lasted only a moment. Vukvun, on the other hand, was just the opposite of his sister. Cheerful, lively, quick-to-laugh, he was a great lover of women. His manly prowess was legendary. And he was not choosy in bed partners – young women or respectable mothers of broods were equally delightful. Caught in the act by a jealous husband or jilted suitor, Vukvun always took the blame and tried to shield his lady of the hour.

Only last night, they had stretched a fresh walrus hide over the roof of the shaman's *yaranga*. It was still somewhat translucent, and the *chottagin* filled with warm yellow light.

The shaman sat upon a walrus vertebra not far from the fire, where there was the most light from the smokehole above. A large, smoothly polished walrus tusk balanced across his knees.

"Amyn etti, Mletkin," Kalyantagrau greeted him kindly, gesturing to another whale vertebra. "Have a seat there."

"What are you going to draw, *epei*?"[1] Mletkin lowered himself comfortably.

1. Chukchi for "grandfather."

In recent times the American traders had started to pay well for painted walrus tusks, which could fetch up to three times the price of raw ones. The gleaming surface of the tusk would usually depict scenes from Luoravetlan life – *yarangas,* sled dog teams, walrus, lakhtak and polar bear hunts. Sometimes carvers would inscribe the reverse with scenes of life in the tundra: reindeer herds, catching and culling deer, conical, portable camp *yarangas.* Or tundra animals such as red and silver foxes, wolves, and birds.

This time, it was a strange, surprising image that took shape on the walrus tusk. A gigantic man held a whale by its fin, looking as if he were about to bite off the whale's head. His huge mouth was full of teeth, but otherwise he looked like a normal man. Looking more closely, Mletkin realized that he was looking at Pichvuchin – a fairy-tale creature in the guise of a human, who could turn into a dwarf or a giant so enormous that he could use the nearest mountaintop for a pillow.

"Recognize him?" said Kalyantagrau, turning the walrus tusk toward the light.

"Yes." Mletkin nodded. "You've drawn him so perfectly, how could I not?"

"And to my mind," Kalyantagrau told him thoughtfully, "the contents of the Sacred Book of the Russians, the one your ancestor brought back from the Anui market fair, are not at all the same as my drawing. It's something else. It's a recording of speech. Not images, but speech! Watch!"

Kalyantagrau brought two crumpled paper wrappers from one of the storerooms. One came from an American packet of loose tea, and the other from a Russian tea brick, hard as a rock, which had to be scraped with a sharp knife.

"Both papers designate one and the same item," Kalyantagrau said. "But the marks are different. You get some that are the same, like this one – A – which looks like the rack for drying pelts. There are similar sounds in human speech, so there's nothing surprising in that. And so we can tell that Tangitan writing is different among the different Tangitan tribes, just as Americans speak one language and Russians speak another."

"If only we could learn to understand the marks!" This was Mletkin's secret wish voiced aloud. He knew that his grandfather Tynemlen had had the same dream.

"First we would need to learn the Tangitan speech," Kalyantagrau told him pointedly.

The shaman poured a little tea into a cup and offered it to his grandson. Mletkin drank the bracing brew with pleasure. He'd been literally run off his feet since morning. Already, he'd jogged up the steep slope to the mouth of the stream, carrying a bundle of metal rods, then down again to the lagoon and back to the village via a boggy tundra path.

Still, sheer physical exertion didn't count for much: the other young men his age – his cousin Atyk, Vamche, another relative, and their young visitor Gemal'kot from faraway Tapkaran – would have been doing much the same. Mental exercise was always the toughest, especially creating incantations on the spur of the moment, being ready for any exigency of life.

"Unlike the Tangitans, we don't have a store of ready-made incantations, set in stone forever," Kalyantagrau had taught. "He who dedicates his life to serving man and Enantomgyn must learn to respond to life's twists and turns with his soul and his reason. And not with just the first words that come to mind, but words that are precise and appropriate to the time and place."

Mletkin already knew that in the future, much would depend on the context of events, but Kalyantagrau never tired of reminding him.

Mletkin always left his shaman grandfather thirsting for solitude and peace. He would ascend the Crag by way of the steepest footpath, and with each step he sensed the horizon widen around him, fill with space and air. From the peak, Uelen's two rows of *yarangas*, strung along the shingled spit, looked just like a walrus-tusk drawing. But Mletkin's eyes wandered out toward Imeklin and Inetlin, the islands in the middle of

Irvytgyr Bay, which looked like a single island from where he perched, so close were they to one another. He would look out at the bluish, barely visible stripe that was the shore of Rochgyn – America – and onward, over the sea's expanse to the north, into an endless unknown.

AT THESE MOMENTS of deep introspection Mletkin sometimes felt as though he had left his body and were looking at himself from outside. Looking at a young man who stood at the edge of a cliff where no other dared to stand. For him – who had trained himself not to fear heights, not to feel dizzy and light-headed as he looked at the ground below, at the white foaming tide and the suddenly minuscule birds and humans – this was no trouble at all. On the edge of the Crag he felt as steady and confident as he did standing atop the level tundra or the surface of a sucking, boggy lake. And if he pushed off gently with his feet, would he stay rooted to the ground or crash to the jagged rockfall littering the slopes below? It was as if he were walking around his corporeal body, peering inside and wondering at the way the regular Uelen Luoravetlan in him merged with a person to whom the secrets of the true nature of things, the commingling and relationships of what seemed like random events, were slowly being revealed. Already he knew how a person's behavior alters with the phases of the moon, how suggestible a person is, how like a child, with a heart that is sensitive and easily wounded. He knew how powerful a plain, single word may be when spoken at the right time, in the right place, and to exactly that person for whom it was meant. "Many people are afraid of the *uivel*, a curse that can be sent across a distance," Kalyantagrau had told him. "I have this power, I can even kill a person in another village. There's no need to send anything material to accomplish this, concentrating strongly on that thought would be enough. I should say though, sometimes it takes me a few days to recover..." "And did you kill many people this way?" asked Mletkin. "A fair number," Kalyantagrau answered calmly, as though they had been speaking of nerpas or lakhtak and not people at all.

Such revelations made the young man uncomfortable, and more than once he had doubts about his chosen path. If a man was given the power to do evil unpunished, would he always be able to use reason to hold back malice, anger, or the desire to harm another? This happens often in life. How many times had Mletkin himself felt it? Now of course he remembered it with a smile, but when his parents had denied him sweet tea or limited his water, many times he had caught himself thinking: I hope they choke on that tea! As he grew up, he began to envy the other boys if they outstripped him in something. And then, instead of trying with all his might to do better, the desire that bubbled up inside him was to see his rival stumble, fall, sprain his foot.

"SO HOW DO you get there?" asked Mletkin that day, as he watched Pichvuchin's heroic deeds come to life on the polished walrus tusk, beneath a sharp, wood-handled awl that looked like a bird's beak.

"Hard to say," Kalyantagrau said after a pause. "One day you will just feel it, you'll know that you can. Something inside will tell you."

"And if it doesn't happen?"

His grandfather put the awl aside and blew the residual bits from the walrus tusk. His answer was slow and measured:

"It will certainly come to you... But I want you to understand, this power is not the most important thing. The main thing is to want to do good. Doing good, helping to ease another's pain and hardship – that is the shaman's chief task. Each of us comes to this life in order to do a small part of Enantomgyn's work. It's as though we humans are all little bits of the Higher Being, we represent him on earth and in this life. And his main concern is to make a person good, worthy."

"But what about the Tangitans?" came Mletkin's burning question.

"All people – Tangitans, Aivanalin, Kaaramkyn, Koryaks, the hairmouths – they are all Enantomgyn's creatures," answered Kalyantagrau.

"So why do they have a different God?"

"There's only one God," the shaman answered. "It's only that they see him in their own way. Different nations speak their own languages, but does that mean that they are not all the same? They are all still human. Human language – regardless of whether it's Russian, American, or our own Lygevetgav[2] – it isn't animal speech, but human."

Mletkin thought of the Tangitans' Sacred Book. Who could teach him Russian? Would he have to volunteer himself into captivity? After all, Daurkin – whom Yakunin's soldiers had captured and taken to their own lands – was taught not only their language but also the skill of marking paper with and recognizing the traces of human speech... Russian speech!

As he contemplated eternity, Mletkin often felt not just estrangement from quotidian life, but more often, an almost unbearable, piercing overflowing of feelings and ideas. There were times when his inner exultation was so strong he wanted to step forward, into the abyss. How he then wanted to soar above the measureless expanse of the sky, to walk on water, or, best of all, to fly like a bird, skimming the foamy waves with his wings! Better still to dissolve into the air, and become not just weightless and invisible but omnipresent, all pervasive.

These moments of turbulent feeling heightened Mletkin's senses, and he could hear voices both near and far as sharply as if they were inside his own head. Birdcalls took on meaning and though it was not human speech he understood it, and marveled that he could. In his mind's eye, he would arc over the horizon and see the neighboring Eskimo village of Nuvuken, beyond the Crag; Rochgyn, the American shore, and its village of Kymgyn, would come through more sharply amid the islands of the strait.

As he neared manhood erotic fantasies began to mingle with Mletkin's visions, sometimes so potent and realistic that they caused him to spill his seed. Every single Uelen beauty had visited Mletkin's

2. Chukchi for "true speech."

dreaming embrace at one time or another and he had to lower his eyes when meeting them, mortified, lest they guess that in his mind he had not only desired but possessed them.

Nowadays he was counted among the hunters. He had killed walrus, polar bear, and whale, not to mention small pinnipeds such as lakhtak and nerpa. He was equally successful in hunting for furs, the chief and most precious goods in the trade with the Tangitans, who would descend from big wooden boats that had gigantic machines hidden deep in their bellies and would trade for whalebone, walrus tusk, hides, and tanned leather, fur-lined clothes. Most of all, though, they wanted Arctic furs and soft fawn skin.

They were also interested in old things – ancient bows and arrows, spears; they might even buy a skin boat. Animal figurines carved from walrus tusk were becoming popular. Kalyantagrau had been the first to start carving whole scenes, such as a nerpa hunt comprising the hunter and the animal, or a boat with its Uelen crew, and many of the tiny figures were recognizable by their faces, deer harnesses, or dogsleds. Kalyantagrau also made walrus-tusk engravings, which he cleverly filled in with ochre and green mud, rubbing the pigment into the outlines to give the image depth and expressiveness.

Mletkin first noticed the ship as it curved around Senlun, a rocky outcrop in the strait. There was no wind, and in the silence and stillness the beating of the enormous metal heart prisoned within the vessel could be heard clearly.

He ran down the Crag to bring the news to his village.

The ship was only just dropping anchor not far from shore, but already the villagers had lowered five boats onto the water. Mletkin rowed with all his might, trying hard to outrun Gemal'kot's boat. Neatly strung bundles of fox, sable, and ermine, decorated fur-lined clothing, packets of whalebone and walrus tusks lay neatly stacked at the bottom of each boat. Apart from these useful goods, almost every hunter also had walrus-tusk figurines of birds and beasts tucked into his coat.

Kalyantagrau, of course, had the richest haul of these. He and Mletkin were the first on deck, joining a screeching, squawking, thrusting crowd that roiled like birds at a breeding ground. Nearly every other man dangled a pungently smoking pipe from his lips; this aromatic smoke was scarce in Uelen due to dwindling tobacco supplies.

This was Mletkin's first time on a Tangitan deck. It was already strewn with the trade items: saws, axes, knives, large and small cauldrons, kettles, packets of tea and tobacco, ten-pound bags of flour, smaller bags of sugar, boxes of army hardtack, colored beads, spools of thread, needles, condensed milk in metal tins, and, slightly off to the side, glinting like dark, sea-bottom ice, bottles of the evil joy-making drink. The same drink also came in small wooden casks.

The Tangitans offered them some of the evil joy-making water from the casks, but only the middle-aged and elderly men drank, and then only a mouthful apiece, as they were well aware of the dangers of losing one's head and getting swept up in foolish trades. After the trading was done, well, that was another matter!

Mletkin picked up two expertly tanned and scraped bearskins, his main winter kills. Sighting the music box, his resolve faltered, and he almost changed his longtime plan to exchange the bearskins for a real Tangitan firearm – an American Winchester.

At first the trading was tumultuous and disorganized. The buyers and sellers – and every man on deck was simultaneously both – dashed about, grabbed items and then dropped them back on deck, chattering at one another loudly and brusquely, as though each understood the other perfectly. A crowd of Tangitans bunched around Kalyantagrau's bone carvings, which he had laid out upon some dark nerpa hides. Snatching at the figurines, they would offer items in trade, everything from bottles of the evil, joy-making water to the hollow beveled needles that were so useful in sewing together tough hides. The shaman stood firm, never accepting the initial offer. All the other goods had a precise, if unwritten, value, but no one could know the true value of the painted walrus tusks.

For a lonely while Mletkin stood beside his bearskins, which were half draped over the side of the boat. Passing sailors glanced enviously at the hides, clacking their tongues appreciatively, as they hurried to the other end of the ship.

Finally, a man fully answering to the description of a hairmouth walked up. His face was covered by a black beard, though it had been shaved in parts. He held a curved pipe between his teeth. The man pinched the hides, weighed each in his hands, ran his hands over the fur and raised an inquisitive glance toward the seller. Mletkin had realized that this was a genuine, serious buyer who, furthermore, knew the goods very well. As to their quality, Mletkin had no fear – they were excellent hides, skinned from mature, full-grown bears, and each a good size.

At last the hairmouth asked the seller to name his price. He said this in his own language, but Mletkin understood him right away. Back home, in preparation for trade, he had drawn a Winchester on a piece of bleached nerpa skin.

The hairmouth glanced at the drawing and burst into a loud peal of laughter, his entire demeanor making it clear that he considered the Luoravetlan's pretensions ridiculous. Amazingly, Mletkin heard the loud stream of words and clucks with almost perfect comprehension. The Tangitan was saying roughly this: "Are you out of your mind? Who's ever seen a savage, who can't manage any weapon but his own bow and arrows and spear, get his hands on a proper firearm? Here, take what you like – tea, sugar, three sacks of flour, five tobacco packets... but a Winchester, you've got to be joking!"

Mletkin put an indifferent, stony look on his face; he even turned his head back to the sea. After the Tangitan had shouted his fill, the young man lifted one of the bearskins slightly to reveal two tightly lashed bundles of extra-long baleen plates propped up against the side of the boat. The Tangitan fell silent and looked back over his shoulder. The rest of the traders stopped their business to observe him and Mletkin. With a final energetic exclamation the Tangitan departed, but soon returned with a small-bore Winchester rifle. Naturally Mletkin would have preferred a different caliber, but this was fine too, good for hunting nerpa and lakhtak in the meltwaters. A set of firing cartridges ought to have come with the gun: Mletkin knew that without ammunition the Tangitan weapon was just a useless metal stick. He explained this through gestures, the Tangitan cursed once more but went to get the cartridges. They fit into the palm of one hand, though the man's palm was largish, the size of a small shovel. Mletkin accepted these but handed over the bearskins only, indicating that the whalebone was staying with him. At the end of a lengthy period of wrangling, Mletkin ended up with a metal box full of cartridges. So as not to turn his luck he retreated back to his boat and stayed there until the end of the day, ignoring the Tangitans' insistent and inviting gestures to return.

By the end of the trading day many of his tribesmen had had a good deal of the evil, joy-making water and fell into their boats like sacks of flour. Both of Mletkin's grandfathers, Tynemlen and Kalyantagrau, were among the well and truly inebriated. Everyone talked loudly, laughing and shouting out Tangitan phrases memorized during the hours on board: Okay! Good! Fak u! Goddam! Hau mach! Wot is cost! Tee! Shuga!

The gaiety continued on shore, as many of the men had purchased glass bottles of the drink, and Gemal'kot even bought a cask of it.

As he watched his cheery kinsmen Mletkin grew anxious: the people he knew were transformed before his eyes. They were losing their habitual calm and self-restraint. Many of the men turned into braggarts, while the women became grief-stricken, burst into tears, and, strangely, would talk nostalgically of the dead, and mourn afresh for those who had been properly mourned long before. Mletkin had sampled the evil joy-making drink himself and even felt a kind of rising spirits at first, but this soon passed, and he found he could not take another mouthful of the drink, it filled him with such revulsion.

On the following morning the Tangitans landed on shore. Laden with their goods and bottles, they made the rounds of the *yarangas*. At first they would treat the inhabitants with drink for free but as soon as they glimpsed some item in the gloom of the *chottagin* they would point to it. They took ancient bows and arrows and quivers, warriors' armor – walrus-tusk plates affixed to nerpa skin or tanned deer hides – spears, and even snowshoes.

Then the *yarangas* rang with the news that the Tangitans took great pleasure in befriending the village women, and that they would pay for this: one man's wife received a generous set of beveled needles, while her husband was rewarded with a bottle...

The Luoravetlan were not without a sense of jealousy, but the Tangitan was considered a creature so far removed from a native Arctic dweller that lying with them did not really amount to marital infidelity.

And it seemed that such "friendships" were not at all unpleasant for Uelen's women; Mletkin suddenly perceived that they were combing their hair, dressing up in special-occasion clothes and ornaments, and washing their faces with urine, which was considered the best cosmetic for toned, smooth skin. Hair sparkled with plaited-through colored spangles, necks were hung with necklaces of glass beads and antique silver Russian coins.

This topsy-turvy life continued for three full days.

Then, one fine morning, the waters off Uelen's shore were empty: the ship had gone. The dogs raised up a loud, ominous howling. All this time they had gone forgotten and unfed, and the hungry dogs had gnawed up several skin boats foolishly left unguarded on the shingled beach. People were beginning to come back to their senses, discovering strange, mysterious objects among the useful and needful items that they had purchased. A gramophone had appeared inside Gemal'kot's *yaranga*. Old Mirgyn walked about the village in a wide cowboy hat while his wife played with a colored parasol, opening and snapping it shut, frightening the children and dogs.

It had been an amazing adventure, which had interrupted the monotonous way of life in Uelen, a way of life that had remained unchanged for centuries. People smiled ruefully, remembering their exploits under the influence of the evil, joy-making water. And they teased old Lonlyh, who had several times rowed his little boat and his old half-blind wife out to the big ship in the hopes of tempting some unfussy Tangitan.

BEFORE THE GREAT yearly walrus hunt at the Inchoun breeding ground, Kalyantagrau delegated the sacrifices and prayers for a good hunt to Mletkin.

The young man already knew whom to address and where to throw the sacrificial offerings. But Kalyantagrau had not told him what words to say; he had only hinted vaguely that if inspiration came from above, so would the right words.

The first light snow of the season was falling, tiny snowflakes that melted as soon as they touched the ground, darkening the shingle and the wet earth, which was scattered with yellowing clumps of grass, to black.

A slow, tenuous dawn was breaking. First, a crimson ribbon pierced through between the waterline and the low dark thunderclouds to the east. The sun was rising unseen, swathed in thick clouds.

Mletkin walked along the shore, reaching down for handfuls of stringy seaweed and popping the soft, wet clumps into his mouth. Finding a piece of tree trunk washed up on shore, he dragged it farther inland and placed a small stone atop it to signify that the item had found an owner.

As he listened closely to the murmuring crash of the tide, Mletkin was attuning himself to that feeling which Kalyantagrau had called inspiration from above. For the moment, though, his heart remained calm and still, and beyond the sea's familiar murmur he could hear nothing. Then a creeping worry came: what would happen if he couldn't speak with the Outer Forces?

Uelen was strung out upon a shingled spit that came to an end with a narrow strait which separated the lagoon from the open sea. Although the stretch of water was hardly twenty footsteps long and less than half that across, the strait was a formidable obstacle. Too deep to walk across, it could not be swum across either: like all his tribesmen, Mletkin couldn't swim. So there was a one-seat hide canoe tethered to a pair of whale jaws at the end of the beach.

When he had stepped up onto the opposite shore Mletkin began to ascend the gradual slope and, by the time he had reached the top of the crags overhanging the walrus breeding ground, dawn had finally fully broken.

His heart was heavy with worry. The thought that he was not fit to be a shaman grew all-pervasive; he briskly dropped the sacrificial foods – this time lumps of sugar, tobacco crumbs, and bits of hardtack – down to the ground, which rang with the noisy incoming tide and the loud grunting and wheezing of hundreds of walrus.

O Great Powers who look down at me from the sky!
Send good fortune to our tribe of Uelen!
Send us good fortune!
Send us good fortune!

Mletkin repeated the last phrase several times but nothing else occurred to him. He spent the entire day waiting for inspiration, above the walrus breeding ground, then returned home moping at twilight.

On the appointed day, the hunters – armed with sharp spears – clambered to the top of the crag, from where they would noiselessly descend and sneak up on the breeding ground.

Mletkin peered down at the shingled beach and reared back in shock and dismay. He almost thought it was a different place, but no, it was just the same beach which every autumn saw walrus herds slide up from the water. But now, aside from a few trampled youngsters, the beach was empty. The walrus had gone.

When they were certain that the herds had left the shingled beach, the grim-eyed hunters made their way back to Uelen. This was a rare occurrence, one that only happened if someone had frightened off the animals: in recent times this would have been the ships full of curious Tangitans.

Mletkin could not look the men full in the face; he pulled his head tightly into his shoulders and walked at a distance from the others.

He entered Kalyantagrau's *yaranga* and stood in its center, in the circle of light that fell from the smokehole onto the earthen floor. The shaman was sitting on a whale vertebra. He greeted his grandson with a stone face.

"I tried," Mletkin hurried to explain. "I said the necessary words and I threw the offering to the East, West, and North, every direction from which animals come to our shores, where the invisible Spirits live..."

"Was there an answer to your incantations?" Kalyantagrau was grave.

"There was no answer," Mletkin answered dejectedly. "I waited, I spoke... but in vain. There was no answer."

"No answer, because you spoke only with your mouth, not with your heart and soul. Because your thoughts were roaming far from this shore, where our livelihood, our good fortune rests... You could not lift your soul sufficiently to speak with the Outer Powers!"

"No," Mletkin confessed. "I couldn't."

"You haven't just shamed yourself, you've brought shame on me as well! Every death from hunger, every child who dies this cold winter will be on your conscience."

"What am I to do then? What am I to do?"

Tears were welling up in his throat. If he were to burst out crying it would complete his disgrace.

"I'll do anything to atone. I'm ready to give my life..."

He had remembered the ancient tale of his ancestor Mlakoran, who had sacrificed his own life and was stabbed to death by his young daughter in order to placate the *rekken*, the evil spirits that brought disease.

"You must leave!" Kalyantagrau's reply was strident and unequivocal. "Go into the tundra, into the mountains, until your soul is cleansed, until you feel yourself changed. And if that does not come to pass, you must leave life itself!"

"What, now?" Mletkin reeled, horror-struck.

"Now!" thundered Kalyantagrau. "Go now!"

In the impenetrable darkness Mletkin trudged slowly along the lagoon, heading toward the mouth of the stream, which in the autumn season of heavy rains swelled and flooded down into the lagoon in full flow. Barely noticing the water, Mletkin crossed the stream and walked upon the boggy tundra floor that slurped and sucked underfoot, up the slope of Linlinney – the Hill of Hearts' Peace.

Something suddenly glimmered up ahead, like a winking flame at the door of a *yaranga*, lit to guide a late-returning hunter home. His heart skipped a beat and a wave of icy horror washed over him. Mletkin halted: was it possible he'd lost his way, and his feet had brought him back to the village? Another step and the possibility vanished as he almost tripped on a human skull, which glowed palely against the dark earth. Mletkin imagined that the glow came from within the bony sphere that once held a living person's brain. Whose skull was this? A burial place was normally marked with a ring of small stones, none bigger than a nerpa's head, but the tundra birds and animals were quick to raid the grave site, mingling the skulls and bones they dug up with those of the long-departed. No one visited Uelen's burial site without a reason. Only in his earliest childhood, walking alongside his grandmother to the berry bushes in the tundra, had Mletkin had to quicken his step and avert his eyes from the blanched skulls, broken sleds, spears, bows, arrows, and the shards of household vessels that accompanied those who had gone beyond the clouds, as they passed along the side of the village graveyard.

Haltingly, barely able to lift his leaden feet from the earth, Mletkin pressed on, stumbling on skeleton parts and the stones that ringed the graves. The camp of the dead seemed better lit than its environs and, to Mletkin, bluish flames seemed to flicker from within the white, luminescent skulls. His heartbeat echoed in his ears with a thundering, resounding toll; a gripping terror froze his guts. A few more steps, and someone powerful, invisible, would grab him by the feet and drag him underground into the depths, where the bad people, unworthy of a place in the sky, eked out their afterlife in tattered, beggarly *yarangas*. Their hunting grounds were scarce of game, so they were always hungry, and always thirsty, too. Kalyantagrau, aided on his shamanic travels by a distillation of the fly agaric mushroom, had sometimes visited this underworld; each time, upon his return, he drank and drank, barely able to assuage a deadly thirst.

An eternity seemed to pass before Mletkin had finally crossed the camp of the dead and embarked on a steep path that led farther into the tundra.

As he left the place of blanched skulls and bones, thoughts of death beat insistently against his brain. According to lore, the dead person left his material body sometime after the funeral. The souls of those who had perished fighting an enemy, those who had dedicated their lives to the good of those they left behind, those who had lived a good life, helping the poor and the orphaned, those souls ascended to the environs around the North Star. There you could see the souls of Mletkin's ancestors – Mlemekym, Mlakoran, Kunleliu – bright among the glittering spray of stars... Why had Kalyantagrau given him the name Mletkin? What did he mean by it? Was he foreseeing his destiny, sensing from afar that his, Mletkin's, lifetime would see the breaking of time? But how would this happen? And why would it happen to him, to Mletkin? If he had felt no divine inspiration then, on the crags above the walrus breeding grounds, surely it meant that he was not destined to ever feel it. And Kalyantagrau's hopes that his grandson would be his successor had been in vain; the shaman had been mistaken.

It must be nice to be one of those who had found their destiny beyond this life. The life of the underworld kingdom may have been full of hardship and pain, but it would flow forever unchangingly. There would be no uncertainty, no false hopes and expectations. It would be the best of all, of course, to be one of those who had flown up to the stars. But there was no place up there for Mletkin, who had consigned his tribesmen to a winter of famine, had failed to placate the Higher Powers.

As he drew farther and farther away from the camp of the dead, his animal terror began to subside, only to be replaced by an equally overwhelming longing for rest. He wanted to sprawl facedown on the earth, arms and legs outflung, to close his eyes and to sink into sleep. Just not here on the cold, waterlogged ground. Up by the little river called Tehyuve'em the incline rose again; there the earth was less damp, and swathes of dried grass and blue-green *vatap*, or deer moss, blanketed the earth.

His thoughts knocked about inside his head, scattering in different directions. If he did not go beyond the clouds, or down to the underworld, would he have the strength to return to his native Uelen, to show his face to his people? Which was the better, death or exile? In his case, it would seem that death was preferable.

He often fell as he stumbled through the darkness. Once, he hit his knee on a jagged stone and a moan of pain escaped him. To his surprise, someone far away responded with a sad, plaintive sound, but it was difficult to tell whether this answering note had come from a human or an animal.

Now it was almost morning. Mletkin could tell by the way the air became more arid, and the way his fevered face felt the occasional gentle breeze, the kind that can rise up even in deep autumn, on the cusp of the first real blizzard of the season, after which the snow does not melt again until spring. It was as though the departed summer were sending back a last whisper of farewell: don't grieve, I will come back again, the warmth of earth and air will return, will hurry back upon the wings of the wind. At last, Mletkin thought he'd found a dry hillock. He ran his hand over the ground and felt the dense carpet of deer moss, which stays dry even in a storm.

Mletkin sprawled on his back, flung his arms and legs akimbo and closed his eyes. It would have been a blessing to forget, to escape the thoughts that were rending his brain, to find a moment of peace. But peace in earnest would come only with death.

Mletkin had always had a particular, not to say unnatural, curiosity about death. Whenever it fell to him to assist Kalyantagrau in helping someone to die, he would peer intently into the dying one's face, and each time he was just as astonished at how little the dead person resembled the living one. Oh, on the outside, the two were similar enough. But only on the outside. It was strikingly apparent that something internal and imperceptible was disappearing, something invisible but so essential that the body of the deceased suddenly seemed no more than a covering, the outer clothing of the person who had now passed into the unfathomable beyond.

Kalyantagrau had confirmed Mletkin's idea that a person's essence, his soul – *kelelvyn* – did not vanish but flew up through the clouds or else fell far down into the underworld, to live a new life, this time for all of eternity.

If Mletkin died, would his soul, too, fly from his earthly body?

A gray autumn day was beginning to dawn, the kind that does not have a sunrise but rather a sudden illumination of everything – the sky, the earth, and the air. Mletkin could now make out his surroundings, the east-facing slope that came gently down the nipple-top of the Pe'eney mountain.

There was no way back. And with the coming of the dawn, he found that he did not want to die. So what if his soul could live on in another world, if there was nothing of this world in that one? Not even this gloomy, unwilling dawn, when nature begins to glow with daylight from within. Nor these unexpected warm breezes, as tender as a mother's hand on your face. There would only be a cold, indifferent world of eternity, but not of life.

Mletkin drifted in and out of a fevered sleep. At times he imagined, in a fever of fright, that his soul had torn away from his body and was soaring over the earth, climbing higher, ever higher.

Night came, and Mletkin still lay in the same spot. He had risen only once, to go down to the stream for a drink of water. So far he had not felt hunger, only an expanding sense of lightness. His soaked clothing had dried during the day, and with the coming of darkness Mletkin once again fell into a dreaming stupor.

The voice came in the middle of the night. It was distinct and clear, though the words seemed to run together in the manner of Tangitan speech. His whole body rigid with attention, Mletkin focused on hearing. Suddenly, in place of Mount Pe'eney's nipple-like peak there was an explosion of pink light. Then the glow changed to blue, and finally, a gigantic visage coalesced, covering fully half the sky.

"We see you!" the words came loud and clear.

Mletkin leaped to his feet. He felt no fear. Rather, he was astonished at the vision and the voice, though not so surprised as to disbelieve them.

"What can I say?" the young man exclaimed.

"You need say nothing!" the voice thundered. "You must act."

MORNING CAME, AND despite the gray dawn and low-hanging clouds, to Mletkin everything around was suffused with an unearthly light, while he himself seemed to see with a different pair of eyes, unclouded, sharp, and farsighted. A glance under his feet revealed each unique blade of grass, each dry, dead flower stem, each pebble as a concrete, particular thing, the way he had seen the world as a child, when he was just beginning to perceive and comprehend it. The vision flickered in and out of his consciousness, but the voice was softer now, less forceful. Mletkin knew that from now on he would be able to call up these visions and voices himself, through an internal effort of will and concentration, and the realization filled him with a sense of freedom, as though some inner set of chains had been loosed. Whenever the visions and voices abated there came in their place a swelling of magical, soul-soothing music – a celestial balm that poured out from invisible, unearthly strings.

Mletkin did not know how long he had spent on the mountainside, by the bank of the Tehyuve'em stream. When he was hungry, he went down to the water's edge and raided the winter supplies of tundra mice; digging up their store-mounds with his bare hands, he extracted the sweet roots they had carefully stockpiled for the coming winter, mentally apologizing to the mice and promising generous recompense, as both his grandmothers and his mother had taught him on their autumn forays into the tundra.

With the first snow, the frost easily penetrated Mletkin's light summer clothes.

He set a course for the deep tundra, leaving behind Mount Pe'eney and the tiny Keniskun camp that straddled the Pacific Ocean shore of the Chukchi Peninsula.

Subsisting on the contents of the mouse store-mounds, the last of the cloud berries, and dug-up yuneu root, Mletkin walked on, charting his way by the stars.

He was very weak when, almost crawling, he managed to cross a half-frozen river and climb onto a high tundra bank, and see before him the white *yarangas* of Rentyrgin, Mletkin's distant blood kinsman, the chief of the deer-people clan Mlakoran had founded so long ago.

First published in Russian: 2000
Translation by Ilona Yazhbin Chavasse

I Have Seen Both Good and Evil
Yevgeny Maximyuk

Natalia Klyucharova's second novel, *Village of Fools* is about a historian named Mitya who goes to a distant village to work as a school teacher. The town is full of all sorts of picturesque characters, several of whom are introduced in this extract. Mitya, however, does not make an appearance in the extracts of the novel published below (the full novel has not been translated into English), and the village referred to in the title is not that in which Father Constantine *et al* live, but one more distant, in a secret location, about which the residents of Mitino are afraid to even think.

Village of Fools

Natalia Klyucharova

Chapter 2
Father Constantine

Father Constantine arrived in Mitino just half a year ago, in winter. He was driven to town by Vova who, since there were no other passengers in the Gazelle minivan, laid into the priest from the moment he arrived in the district capital, asking that he sit in the front passenger seat, so that he could spend the entire drive peppering him with theological questions.

For instance, Vova was curious to know which saint to address his prayers to, in order to win back a *certain bitch*? Or did saints not concern themselves with such things, and would he then have to dash off to Maryino, to the old woman and her potions, which of course he did not want to do – always jacking up the price, the witch was, charging you half your paycheck for a glass of dried up dung!

Vova also asked whether one should remove the cross he wore around his neck when he was *doing it with a girl*? And, to keep from going to Hell, was it enough to go to church at Easter, or did *one also have to attend Christmas services as well*?

"That is all irrelevant," Father Constantine finally said, no longer able to restrain himself, an answer which greatly surprised – which is not to say disappointed – Vova.

"Then whattya gotta do?"

"Live decently. Day to day, you understand, and not just light a candle once a year."

"By the way," Vova replied, inspired because he sensed the conversation moving back into familiar terrain. "Is it true that you shouldn't light an even number of candles or you'll kick the bucket?"

"Of course you'll kick it. Sooner or later. But not because of candles."

Vova went silent. His face expressed the physical exertion brought on by thinking: wrinkled brow, frosted eyebrows frowning – twitching as if pushing out a stuck thought, muscles knotted.

"So you're saying I don't live decently?" he blurted out, offended. "I drink, by the way, only in the evening, and not in the morning, like everyone else. Although, of course, the hair of the dog does tempt me. I suffer so; I slave like an elk. But I never drink and drive, that's ironclad."

"Certainly you don't drink *every* day, without a rest?" Father Constantine asked, his voice expressing the sort of concern one might have were they talking about a serious illness, rather than about a common pursuit.

"Well, yeah," Vova said, surprised. "How else?"

"Look, you asked me what you should do," Father Constantine sighed, knowing well in advance that the words he had to say would have no effect.

"Yeah," Vova replied, "I don't wanna end up in Hell."

"Well, why don't you try, for a start, drinking maybe just every other day. When you can do that, come and see me, and I will tell you what's next."

"Aha," Vova grinned, "Don't I know what's next: drink only on Fridays, then only on holidays, then chemical implants. So that everyone would be pointing their fingers at me, like some sectarian! No thanks. It's envy made you blurt that out, little father. What, are you priests banned from putting it behind the collar? Hm, did I guess it?"

"Why banned? All things are lawful. But not all things are expedient."

"The hell! So *I'm* not supposed to drink, but for *you* all things are lawful!"

"No, Vova," Father Constantine wearily explained, infinitely sorry that he had gotten himself involved in this conversation. "It is a phrase from St. Paul. It applies to all, not just to the priesthood."

"So that means it's lawful for me?" Vova exulted.

"But it is also not expedient for you."

"Well, yeah. No one's gonna argue with that," Vova agreed, relieved. Then he excitedly began to recount how he had been poisoned by aviation fluid, something that happened – as all important things in Vova's life – when he was in the military.

ENTERING THE UNHEATED rectory, which in its size and frailty resembled a wooden shack, Father Constantine – without removing his winter coat – sat down at the table and inscribed in his diary:

What can one do to inherit eternal life? In Judea in the 1st century, the answer was: 'Forsake all that you have and follow me.' And that was too much. In Russia in the 21st century the answer is: 'Drink just every other day.' And that is also too much. You always ask too much. Would it not be easier to simply say: such and such number of candles?

Father Constantine surveyed the hoarfrost-coated walls of his new residence, the rattling window pane patched with cellophane tape, Lenin's lightbulb[1] swinging from a long cord, and thought that he had every reason to lapse into a depression. But he knew it would not be expedient.

MEANWHILE, VOVA WAS holding forth on the porch of the store, brandishing an open bottle.

1. "*Lampochka Ilyicha*" – an expression dating to Lenin's push for electificiation, connoting a bare, naked bulb without any sort of fixture.

"He didn't impress me. A troubled sort. Don't go to church, he says, drink all you want. Although it's harmful, of course."

"Maybe he's a fake? Not a priest?" queried the gloomy Pakhomov, who had once been a tractor-driver.

"Maybe even a fake. I didn't ask to see his documents."

"Too bad!" Gavrilov the pensioner chided as he exited the store. Everyone knew that Gavrilov was a stoolpigeon and a troublemaker.

Gavrilov didn't drink with the *muzhiks*, but carried home a kilo of wieners.

"How was I to know," Vova snapped, annoyed that he had fallen into a trap. "I thought, 'he's wearin' a dress, must be a priest.'"

"Well, c'mon, don't hog it," the reticent Pakhomov said, interrupting him.

Vova took a quick gulp, grunted, and passed the bottle to the next in line.

THE NEXT MORNING, Father Constantine also headed to the store, intending to purchase something for his uninhabited shack of a house. Anything, even the simplest thing, could insert a sense of human presence between its dreary walls, easing his transplantation into this new place. A soap dish, a mug, a straw broom.

On the bench near the store, slumping into one another, Vova's companions drowsed. Clouds of icy steam poured out of their dreadful, gaping mouths. Thus did Father Constantine discern that they were alive, although, judging by the small snowdrifts atop their shoulders and the napes of their necks, they had slept here all night.

A small gathering had assembled inside the store. A salesgirl, who had delicate violet highlights in her hair, filled in a crossword. The pensioner Gavrilov fussily examined frozen chicken claws that, due to his thriftiness, he fed to his dog. Nearby, supported by the counter, rocking slightly back and forth, was a young woman in a bright orange railway vest from God knows where, given that the nearest train station was 200 kilometers away.

"Come, grampa, come on, you old stump," she said slowly and hoarsely, "I'm not askin' you for vodka, but for bread. Buy a loaf, it won't break you. Two days I haven't had a bite."

Pensioner Gavrilov, fastidiously pursing his lips, tossed some bluish avian claws into his plastic bag.

"Well, clearly you're no good – feeding your guard dog with frozen claws," the woman laughed and then noticed the new customer. "Queen of Heaven, what sort of deity is this?"

The salesgirl and pensioner tore themselves away from what they were doing and fixed their gaze on Father Constantine.

"Ah, so we heard, we heard," Gavrilov said, instantly finding his bearings. "We love the Church, respect it. On holidays we don't clean our homes, don't cook, just sit in front of the TV all day. Everything as it should be."

"Holy angel, buy a widow a quarter-liter!" the woman in the vest butted in.

"Lyubka, don't pester," the salesgirl hissed.

"What of it? He should help the poor!"

"And how exactly are you a widow?" the pensioner Gavrilov asked, attacking Lyubka. "The seven Tadzhiks from the sawmill? The loonies from the village? They're all still alive! You lascivious vixen!"

"I'm widow of all the dead," Lyubka pronounced meaningfully, herself surprised at how smoothly the phrase came out.

Pensioner Gavrilov paid for his chicken claws, promised Father Constantine he would pop by in the evening for a visit, and retired with dignity.

Father Constantine looked over the coils of rope, the shears and galoshes spread out in the hardware section, and could not for the life of him remember why he had come.

"May I help you?" the salesgirl asked with pointed politeness.

"Yes, please, some bread."

"–and circus!" Lyubka snorted, whirling about the store, imitating a circus dancer.

Father Constantine extended the damp loaf toward her. Lyubka stopped, as if transfixed, while a naughty grin danced about her face.

"For me?" she asked, dumbfounded.

"Well, you asked for it."

"Take a little sausage too," the salesgirl prompted. "That one lives on spirits alone, like a perpetual motion machine."

FATHER CONSTANTINE LEFT the store. Lyubka did not leave his side. Clasping to her chest the plastic bag containing her miraculously acquired provisions, she conversed about something that, by her reckoning, rivaled the solemnity of the occasion.

"God sent the vixen a piece of bread!" Lyubka cried out. "And I don't believe in God. I believe in people. In you, for example. Help a poor widow! That's how we live. Just as you've decided to give up the ghost, bam! A crumb from heaven. Live on, then, Lyubka! How can one not believe in God! I believe! God is my witness! And you, so miraculous, just like a saint! You're not a saint by chance?"

"No, Lyuba, just a normal person."

"Oy," Lyubka cried, moved. "Lyuba! Oh, say it again! No one ever calls me that!"

The *muzhiks* on the bench were roused by Lyubka's cries.

"What did I say? A fake," the gloomy Pakhomov croaked. "Already collaborating with the psycho. Would a decent man hang out with her? Or talk to her? Only language she understands is the fist."

"Where was it Vovchik saw such scrawny priests? In his army was it?" said his drinking buddy Palych, spouse of Yevdokia, the school headmistress. "A priest should have a pot belly. And this one! He's a crane! Definitely a fake!"

Lyubka chattered on. "Would you like to come for a visit? I do have a house, you know! True, the windows are broken, but the roof is still in place. Or are women off limits for you spiritual folk? Ha-ha-ha! Don't be offended. I'm just joking; I understand everything! C'mon, let's go, you can see how we live here! Or maybe you're squeamish?"

"Let's go."

"Really? You're not joking? To my place? To Lyubka's? What a trick!"

They approached a hovel that listed to one side. Virgin snow hung on the half-opened door. Lyubka had long since recalled that she had a home.

"Who broke your window?" Father Constantine asked.

"The womenfolk!" Lyubka said, cheerfully waving it off. "Because the *muzhiks* keep company with me. And why shouldn't they? I'm a woman of loose morals! And a wife is like a circular saw – she doesn't rest until she's sawn clean through."

With some difficulty they squeezed through the frozen door and went inside. Father Constantine had never seen such mayhem, not even in the houses marked for demolition where, as a child, he would search for treasure.

He stepped over piles of junk and empty bottles.

"A bit untidy," Lyubka noted guiltily, kicking aside an empty box as she passed.

A plastic rattle lay on the windowsill, dusted with snow. Father Constantine picked it up and turned to Lyubka.

"I had a son," she winced miserably. "They took him off to the orphanage. And I loved him so! Sometimes I would forget to feed him, and he would cry, such a muddle. He'd be quiet, if we lived together now."

For the first time since they had become acquainted, Lyubka fell silent, as if lost in thought. Her weathered face, constantly in motion, stopped, and it was suddenly eclipsed by human features: a pointed nose, tiny freckles that were a shade of deathly grey in the scant light collected through the broken window. Her eyes were indeed like those of a vixen: yellowish-brown, cold.

"Do you like me?" Lyubka tossed out, squirming inside her dimensionless orange vest with something like animal coquettishness. "Oh, sorry! So young and already spiritual! Ah you and I could really have started a fire! I sense a kindred spirit in you! God is my witness! It's as if we've known each other 100 years!"

Father Constantine replaced the rattle and carefully started to make his way into the second room, which, judging from certain residual evidence, might once have been called a kitchen. There, he found something quite unbelievable.

"Lyub!"

Lyubka dropped the rattle, which she had been shaking with deaf persistence near her ear, and rushed to the summons.

"Lyub, what is this?"

Lyubka foolishly raised her eyebrows and stared.

"He needs to ask! Can't you see? Shit!"

"How can I *not* see. But why is it right here? Shame on you!"

"Well, there is a bit," Lyubka said, becoming confused, then suddenly beamed. "But you get me some hooch and the shame will disappear! C'mon, angel, c'mon now, holy of holies, if you're so good, buy me something to drink."

"Lyub, it is a good thing that you are ashamed. It is bad when there is no shame."

"Well, that's it – put on his sombrero," Lyuka said, sagging.

"What?"

"That's what I'm saying. It's all sombrero. Big words from complicated books. Way over my head."

Father Constantine sighed.

"So, you're not gonna buy any?" Lyubka clarified.

"No, Lyuba, I will never buy alcohol for you. Please do not ever forget this."

"Well then, commander," Lyubka said, wrapping her vest tight around her and making her way to the exit with a royal air. "Then I have no need for you. I'll seek out generous admirers elsewhere."

RETURNING TO HIS shack, Father Constantine opened his diary, breathed for a long time on his frozen pen, frowned, thought hard and in the end wrote down just two words: "Extremely dreadful."

Chapter Six
Kostya

"It's a miracle!" Claudia Ivanovna cried out, running into the room, in the sort of throat-filling voice with which one yells "Fire!"

Father Constantine steeled himself. In the week since he had arrived in Mitino he had been fortunate enough to witness a few of Claudia Ivanovna's miracles. The first was when she dreamed that Pakhomov went on a bender. And, the next day, sure enough he drank himself into a stupor! Father Constantine, who had never seen the former tractor driver sober, allowed himself to doubt Claudia Ivanovna's prophetic gift, for which he was definitively recorded (in the pensioner Gavrilov's hand) as a "dangerous modernist."

The next day, the primary school teacher saw the profile of Archangel Gabriel in the clouds, but that was only the half of it. The church's dilapidated roof sprung a leak during the spring thaw. Father Constantine climbed up with a bit of roofing felt, and Claudia, seeing the door of the church open on her way home, stopped in to light a candle and her triumphant scream alerted the world and the clergy to the miracle of a weeping icon. Several drops from the leaky roof had fallen on the frame of the sooty icon of Saint Panteleimon the Healer.

And thus did the new miracle arise.

"A runaway from the orphanage showed up at school today," Claudia Ivanovna enthusiastically reported. "He turned everything upside down. But that's not important. We lured him into the dining room with soup then locked him up. He did irreparable damage, of course. But again, that's not important. So while he was in there banging away, we called to the orphanage. And you know who they said this little scoundrel was? Our

Lyubka's son! A miracle! They took him away when he was three months old! And he blundered to this very place! A miracle!"

"Where is he now?"

"They deported him back there," Claudia Ivanovna said, brushing the matter aside. "But truly, it's unbelievable, that he would run to the exact place where he was born! Why are you so quiet? Are you doubting again?"

"I believe he knew where he was running to," Father Constantine admitted, though he would have preferred to dodge her question with silence.

"You are such a Doubting Thomas," Claudia Ivanovna said with dismay. "How is it they ever let you into the priesthood?"

THE NEXT DAY Father Constantine saw bicycles lying in the spongy snow outside the store. The group of seven Tadzhiks had come from the sawmill to buy some ramen noodles. They only ever showed up in the village together, and only when their situation *vis-a-vis* provisions was particularly dire. As Nina the violet salesgirl explained it to Father Constantine, the Tadzhiks were deathly afraid of Vovka, who, while in the army, had acquired an enduring hatred for "sabre-toothed *churki*,"[2] and beat up on all of them indiscriminately.

Lyubka, who had gone missing since the day she and Father Constantine were first acquainted, was hovering about near the bicycles. She was in a fighting mood: chopping at the air with her palm, shaking her fist at the empty street and passionately quarreling with an invisible companion.

As the Tadzhiks were filing out of the store one after the other, Lyubka noticed Father Constantine.

"Aha, most holy!" she keened, and the Tadzhiks scuttled onto their bicycles. "So you think that Lyubka is not a person?"

"I do not."

2. *churki* – a derogatory term referring to illegal migrants from former USSR republics.

"But Lyubka *is* a person! And *churki* are persons!" She waved her arms in the direction of the successfully escaping Tadzhiks. "But no one believes it."

"I do."

"You? The hell you do! As if I could forget. Psycho! Lascivious vixen! Who am I!"

"A person."

"Get on!" Lyubka scowled, then turned away.

Father Constantine hesitated for a moment, thinking that by all appearances their conversation had ended. But then Lyubka looked back over her shoulder and said tearfully, "They took my daughter away from me. And I turned rotten. Had I only looked into her clear little eyes, I might have held myself together…"

"You mean to say you had two? Two children?"

"Naw, just one. Such a wee thing, but when she cried you had to stop up your ears!"

"But that was your son!"

"Son? Well, maybe so. It was so long ago."

FATHER CONSTANTINE WAS overtaken by a panting Yevdokia Pavlovna before he reached his house.

"Batyushka, please help! I can't find a man anywhere! They've all gone off to Pustoye Rozhdestvo![3] To a wedding party!"

"What's the matter?"

"Help us catch the boy!"

"The one from yesterday?" Father Constantine said, clarifying the point as he turned to follow.

"Yes, yes! He returned! What will we do now? He's gonna rip us to shreds!"

3. Pustoye Rozhdestvo – the name of the village is literally, "Empty Christmas."

There was such a hue and cry coming out of the Mitino school, you would think a brigade of lumberjacks was working inside.

"We sent all the children home, for their protection," a frightened Yevdokia Pavlovna explained. "Claudia Ivanovna locked herself in the teacher's room. I ran to get help."

"You go into the teacher's room as well," Father Constantine ordered.

Yevdokia Pavlovka slipped through the door, turned the lock, and something heavy, most likely the director's desk, scraped across the floor.

Father Constantine found the raging boy in the very first room. Wrapped in a curtain, he was hopping across the desks, banging a ladle against an aluminum pot from the cafeteria. He was sporting a second, smaller pot, emblazoned with the word "Compote," on his head. The remains of chairs and dirt from upturned flowerpots lay near the blackboard.

When he saw Father Constantine, the runaway orphan had the most unexpected reaction. He tore off all his gear, jumped off the desk, ran up to him, wrapped both arms around him, buried his face, and froze. In the sudden silence, the discarded pot made a long, lonely roll across the floor until, finally, it crashed into the wall.

Without releasing his grip, the boy raised his freckle-covered, sharp-nosed face and flashed a charming smile. Lyubka's cold eyes stared back at Father Constantine. As an afterthought, the orphan batted his thick eyelashes and smiled wider still.

"What's your name?" he asked with mock childishness.

"Father Constantine."

"And I am Kostya![4] Can I come live with you?"

"Let's go."

They left the demolished room. Without taking his grip off Father Constantine, Kostya turned and kicked the door of the teacher's room as they passed, "Hey, hens! Out with you! The siege is ended!"

4. Kostya is a diminutive for Constantine.

That evening, Father Constantine went to visit Yevdokia Pavlovna. Despite the late hour, work was in full swing at the school. Three tenth-graders were uprighting the desks overturned by the puny Kostya, girls were cleaning the floors, and Claudia Ivanovna was drinking Corvalol[5] and vowing revenge. Auntie Dunya[6] bustled about amid the chaos brought on by the runaway orphan, not knowing what to do with herself.

Father Constantine went into the teacher's room in order to discuss Kostya's future fate. As he had expected, the female pedagogues fully intended to return the little thug to the orphanage. In fact, they would have long since called for a car to be sent from there, but the clever boy had cut the telephone line, and there was no cell service in Mitino.

"But he would just return again tomorrow," Father Constantine said. "And you could be sure that then he would not leave one stone standing upon another. In retaliation."

"Then what should we do?" Yevdokia Pavlovna asked, clearly scared.

"Don't call them just yet."

"How then…?" Claudia Ivanovna began indignantly.

"Let him meet his mother," Father Constantine proposed, looking directly into the timid, inquisitive eyes of the young school director. "Then things will be clearer. Maybe he would then return to the orphanage of his own accord. So long as he has a goal, he will come running here, and each time he will be wilder than the last."

"Never!" Claudia Ivanova finally said, standing up. "We will call and request that they send him somewhere farther away. To a neuro-psychiatric unit. That's just the place for him!"

"For what? Because the child wanted to see his mother for once in his life?" Yevdokia Pavlovna unexpectedly interjected.

The scales tilted. Kostya was allowed to remain in his native village.

5. Corvalol is a barbiturate-based heart medication and a mild tranquilizer, popular in Russia, the former Soviet Union and Eastern Europe. While considered a normal, safe over-the-counter drug there, it contains barbiturates and is a controlled substance that cannot be brought into the U.S.

6. Dunya is a diminutive for Yevdokia.

WHEN HE RETURNED, Father Constantine found his wretched quarters turned upside down. The sink was ripped from the wall, the soap was crushed underfoot, his recently purchased cup was broken, the spoon was tied in a knot, and feathers from a gutted pillow were flying about everywhere. Kostya was lying, stretched out across the bed, watching him coldly.

Father Constantine walked across the floor of the shack, saw in the corner his busted up chair, and touched the top of the oak table.

"Why did you not destroy the table?" he asked. "Ran out of steam?"

"Took a breather!" Kostya smiled widely, without, however, softening his gaze.

"So, even you get tired."

Father Constantine sat on the edge of the bed, thoughtfully extracted a white feather from his beard and sadly said, "Well, Kostya, it will not be easy for you to meet your mother. She is almost never at home. I stopped in just now and it was empty. If you like, we can go there and you can see where she lives. Her door is always open."

"No! I don't want to!" Kostya said fearfully.

For a few seconds, his face convulsed, not knowing what expression to put on. Father Constantine stood and went over to the window. Little Kostya, frantically clenching his teeth, cried like a grown-up.

Meanwhile, pensioner Gavrilov made a new entry into his dossier: *"He is sheltering a runaway criminal!"* Taking pleasure in his accomplishment, he sighed and with deep sorrow inserted the adjective *"under-aged."* Pensioner Gavrilov was an honest citizen.

FATHER CONSTANTINE DID not know where to look for Lyubka, whose life for the most part proceeded beyond the bounds of the village that despised her. But the next morning, heading out to the store to buy a cup and some food for Kostya, he saw the familiar orange vest at the fence outside the church.

Lyubka stood in a melting snowbank, hanging onto the iron bars, eagerly staring at the churchyard. Hearing footsteps, she turned around, and

Father Constantine was struck by how her face had become suddenly more intelligent.

"Is it true?" Lyubka asked, in a voice that held not a shadow of the previous day's dementia.

"Yes."

"And how is he?"

"He's sleeping. If you like, you can go in."

"No! I don't want to!" Lyuba said in horror, exactly mimicking Kostya from the night before. Father Constantine feared that she would also now break out crying.

But she held herself together and walked to the store with him.

Father Constantine bought sausages and bread.

"You damned fool!" Lyubka said on the porch, flinging up her hands. "Who would feed a kid like this! He needs milk! Pas-ture-iz-ed!"

"Lyub, he's ten years old. Milk no longer fills him up."

"Ten?!" Lyubka gasped, not saying another word the rest of the way back to the church.

LYUBKA AGAIN REFUSED to enter the shack where the unknown ten-year-old child slept, the child who, in her head at least, was still a squealing infant.

"I will go and get things ready," she said, gesturing vaguely in the direction of her house.

"Now don't you drink," Father Constantine implored, without any measure of hope.

"No, no!" Lyubka said suddenly, "As if I know nothing!"

THE BOY WAS not in the shack. Father Constantine put away the groceries and began to quietly eliminate traces of the previous evening's mayhem. A half hour later, after he had re-fastened the sink, he heard from behind him: "By the way, in the future I also wouldn't say no to milk."

Kostya was sitting on the table, gripping the loaf and the sausage, fiercely biting one, then the other. In his savage habits, however, there was no longer the sense of a man flying upside down. His expression had subtly changed, as if within him there had appeared a small island of peace, as if Kostya, who had been going about in the world without rudder or sail, had found a straw and had grasped onto it.

Father Constantine understood that they had met, but he did not attempt to ask about it. Kostya also did not consider it necessary to fill him in on any details. He ate his fill, crammed the remaining end pieces into the pockets of his dirty orphanage jacket, jumped down off the table and slipped out the door without saying goodbye.

Father Constantine wanted to get back to his repair work, but could not find the hammer nor the can of nails that he had left on the stool underneath the sink.

IN THE EVENING, Yevdokia Pavlovna looked in on him.

"He covered Lyubka's window with plywood," the diminutive director said, looking inquisitively at Father Constantine, as if she did not know how she was supposed to react to what had happened.

"Well, we'll see," he said. "Just don't call anywhere, please."

"The *muzhiks* are still at the wedding," Dunya sighed, foreseeing a frightful reunion with a husband who had been on a weeklong bender. "The telephone is still not working. But you know that as soon as it's fixed, Claudia will immediately call.

At these final words, Yevdokia, thinking not about the phone, but about her insufferable personal life, unexpectedly broke down crying.

"If you only knew. If only you knew!" she bawled helplessly, the tears pouring out of her.

Father Constantine sat next to her, and Dunya buried her face in his shoulder, like a child, sobbing with all her being.

THE NEXT MORNING, Father Constantine headed off to the orphanage from which Kostya had escaped. He needed to beat Claudia Ivanovna to the punch. He went on foot, occasionally breaking into a jog to warm up. Vova the chauffeur, despite his ironclad vow to never drink in the morning, had also gone missing at the wedding in Pustoye Rozhdestvo. In fact, it was one of his army buddies that had gotten married.

It wasn't far to the orphanage, just 20 kilometers. And by lunchtime, Father Constantine was sitting in the director's office, explaining the situation over and over again. Seeing the soft, good-natured face of Olga Vladilenovna,[7] the head of the children's home, he concluded that there was hope. And he was not mistaken.

When the negotiations stretched into their second hour, and the secretary, burning up with curiosity, came in to take away the tray of untouched tea, a frowning Olga Vladilenovna began to give in. Father Constantine, who by this time had used up all his arguments, was horrified that his strength might not suffice to exert the final, tiny bit of effort required.

But at that very moment the directress herself came to his aid.

"Is it true what they say," she asked, lowering her voice as if voicing a secret, "that the end of the world is near?"

Having no strength to contradict her, Father Constantine nodded in defeat.

"Okay, then, let him be," Olga agreed superstitiously. "Why not? For now we'll list him among the runaways. And if things work out there, we'll restore him to his mother. A one-time thing."

LATE IN THE evening, returning to Mitino, Father Constantine was surprised to see the windows of the school aglow. Little Yevdokia sat in the teacher's room. Seeing Father Constantine, she hurriedly applied a handkerchief to a bruise under her eye.

"I fell," Dunya clumsily lied, looking away. "Everything froze, and it's so slippery. And I was doing a bit of work. So much to do. Thank you for everything. Good night!"

7. The director's patronymic is derived from her father's name, Vladilen – a revolutionary name that was created from a contraction of Vladimir and Lenin.

The *muzhiks*, having returned from the wedding, were buzzing about the closed store. Palych, little Yevdokia's husband, punched the air with his fist, agitating the others to go visit the moonshiner Alka. Vovka, who nonetheless planned to go to work the next day, vaguely protested. Gloomy Pakhomov held his tongue, contemplating a stationary thought.

"Kuzma Palych," Father Constantine called out.

The fist froze and slowly descended. Palych, knocked out of his fighter's rhythm, lapsed into his tearful, good-natured phase.

"Batushka," he said pleasantly. "Look at you! Wandering about at night like a mere mortal!"

"Kuzma Palych, do you beat your wife?"

"I do," Palych said with an inexpressible bitterness. "I beat her, father! If you don't knock, you don't get in!"

A WEEK OF relative peace followed, not counting the daily scandals on the part of the wounded Claudia Ivanovna. On the quiet, Pensioner Gavrilov composed and sent his first anonymous letter to the eparchy, written in a style that left him feeling very pleased.

His terse denunciation recounted the story of Lyubka and Kostya and, with utmost propriety, albeit sarcastically, he pointed out the incompatibility of Father Constantine's calling and the sheltering of *a loose woman and a runaway thief.*

February ended, and the air was filled with the aroma of spring. One morning Father Constantine looked out his window and spied the first rooks. They were walking about self-importantly on a thawed patch in front of the wicket-gate, and reluctantly flew off when a disheveled Lyubka burst into the yard.

"I give up!" she cried out from the threshold. "Someone save me!"

"What?"

"Just don't tell me that I have to be patient! I have put up with all I can. That's it, it's not gonna work!"

"It's not working with Kostya?"

"He's got nothing to do with it. The problem's with me. I need to drink or I will die. I'm not joking."

"Lyuba..."

"To hell with your 'Lyuba'! Now you're gonna start your song about how he's my last chance, that if I cut loose, they'll take him again, and I'll die in the gutter! I know! To hell with it! I've gotta drink. Do you understand me or no?"

"Well you are *his* last chance."

"I know," Lyubka replied, a bit quieter. "What am I to do? I'm still going."

"Where?"

"Why, to the sawmill. The Tadzhiks are good guys. And they offer me spirits."

"So do you really need *muzhiks* or drink?"

"You wish!" Lyubka snorted. "If I had money, I would be cultured, like a rich woman, and take my treatment at home. I'm not in this for the fun. There's something inside me fighting against my head. I understand everything, and it's bringing me down."

"Can you really do it like that, alone? Without companionship?"

"Any fool knows that. I'm an alcoholic after all."

"Ok, Lyub. I will buy it for you myself, if that's how it is. And I will temporarily take Kostya. And when you are yourself again, come and get him."

"You, for me?" Lyubka smiled, incredulous. "You're something, holy one! I never expected it!"

"But only on the condition that you, honestly, do not go anywhere."

"No-no! You can lock me up if you don't believe me."

THUS BEGAN THEIR strange, frail life, not unlike a house of cards. For a week, Lyubka and her son would live almost like a normal family. Shovel the debris from their home, attempt to sort out some sort of life.

Then Lyubka would come running to Father Constantine, as if scalded, and he would walk silently to the store, then she would be locked up alone in her hovel for several days. And Kostya, who no longer destroyed things, moved into the shack next to the church.

A little while later, Lyubka's crisis would come to an end, and, guiltily hiccupping, she would come and retrieve her son.

At Father Constantine's request, Kostya even tried attending school. True enough, he quickly gave it up, declaring that he *did not respect a single one of those hens.*

Some of their neighbors began to help the phantom family out a bit. The salesgirl Ninka agreed to give Lyubka goods that had been written off as sub-standard: broken macaroni, rock-hard cookies and water-logged tea. Blissful Serafima knitted Kosya a scarf and socks, and started on a cap. The plain-looking tenth-grader Sanya helped replace the glass in the window and brought over a novel for them to read called *Poor Folk.*[8]

"It's all nonsense," Kostya concluded, leafing through the tattered pages. "A guy and his chick live in neighboring houses. And all they do is write each other letters. As if they were too lazy to walk next door."

"So it's about love?" Lyubka said, livening up.

"Naw. Total brainwashing."

First published in Russian: 2010
Translation by Paul E. Richardson

8. Fyodor Dostoyevsky's first novel, published in 1846.

Игра

Зинаида Гиппиус

Совсем не плох и спуск с горы:
Кто бури знал, тот мудрость ценит.
Лишь одного мне жаль: игры...
Ее и мудрость не заменит.

Игра загадочней всего
И бескорыстнее на свете.
Она всегда – ни для чего,
Как ни над чем смеются дети.

Котенок возится с клубком,
Играет море в постоянство...
И всякий ведал – за рулем –
Игру бездумную с пространством.

Играет с рифмами поэт,
И пена – по краям бокала...
А здесь, на спуске, разве след –
След от игры остался малый.

Play

Zinaida Gippius

It's not so bad – this downhill way:
Those who've known storms prize wisdom duly.
I'll only miss the sense of play...
For wisdom can't replace it, truly.

Nobody knows why play evolved,
To serve what purpose – it's mysterious.
True play's a riddle still unsolved.
Kids play for fun, but fun is serious.

The kitten plays with yarn or wool;
The waves all caper in the ocean;
And in our cars we feel the pull
To play with speed and space and motion.

We poets play around with rhyme.
Just watch the foam play on champagne!
But I'm on life's wise downhill climb
Where one looks for play in vain.

First published in Russian, 1900
Translation by Lydia Razran Stone